E·S·S·E·N·T·I·A·L·L·Y
TURKEY

D0313669

FORTHCOMING TITLES IN THIS SERIES

E·S·S·E·N·T·I·A·L·L·Y
TURKEY

CAROLE & CHRIS STEWART

CHRISTOPHER HELM
London

© 1987 Carole and Chris Stewart

Reprinted 1987

Line drawings by Kate Osborne

Christopher Helm (Publishers) Ltd, Imperial House,
21–25 North Street, Bromley, Kent BR1 1SD

British Library Cataloguing in Publication Data

Stewart, Carole
  Essentially Turkey.
  1. Turkey — Description and travel—
  Guide-books
  I. Title   II. Stewart, Chris
  915.61′0438   DR416

ISBN 0–7470–3003–0

Phototypeset by Opus, Oxford
Printed and bound by The Guernsey Press Co. Ltd.,
Guernsey, Channel Islands.

C·O·N·T·E·N·T·S

M·A·P

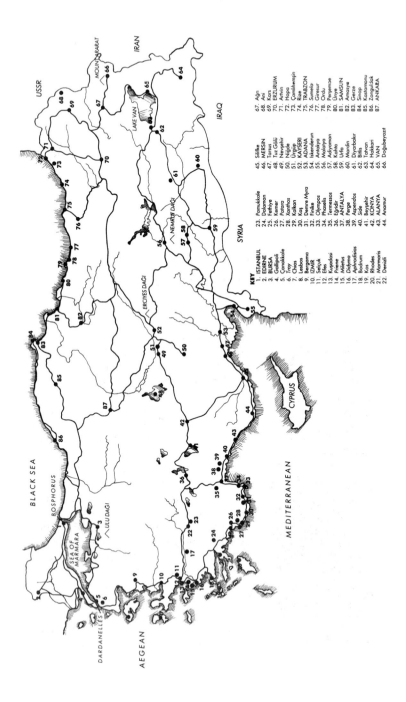

KEY

1. ISTANBUL
2. EDIRNE
3. BURSA
4. Çanakkale
5. Gallipoli
6. Troy
7. Chios
8. Lesbos
9. Bergama
10. IZMIR
11. Selçuk
12. Efes
13. Kuşadası
14. Priene
15. Miletus
16. Didyma
17. Aphrodisias
18. Bodrum
19. Kos
20. Rhodes
21. Marmaris
22. Denizli
23. Pamukkale
24. Dalaman
25. Fethiye
26. Kemer
27. Patara
28. Xanthos
29. Kalkan
30. Kaş
31. Demre Myra
32. Finike
33. Olympos
34. Phaselis
35. Termessos
36. Eğridir
37. ANTALYA
38. Perge
39. Aspendos
40. Side
41. Beyşehir
42. KONYA
43. ALANYA
44. Anamur
45. Silifke
46. MERSIN
47. Tarsus
48. Tuz Gölü
49. Nevşehir
50. Niğde
51. Ürgüp
52. KAYSERI
53. ADANA
54. Iskenderun
55. Antakya
56. Malatya
57. Adıyaman
58. Kahta
59. Urfa
60. Mardin
61. Diyarbakır
62. Bitlis
63. Tatvan
64. Hakkari
65. VAN
66. Doğubeyazıt
67. Ağrı
68. Ani
69. Kars
70. ERZURUM
71. Artvin
72. Hopa
73. Çamlıhemşin
74. Rize
75. TRABZON
76. Sümela
77. Giresun
78. Ordu
79. Perşembe
80. Ünye
81. SAMSUN
82. Amasya
83. Gerze
84. Sinop
85. Kastamonu
86. Zonguldak
87. ANKARA

I·N·T·R·O·D·U·C·T·I·O·N

The holiday destinations of the last decade or so are beginning to lose their novelty; many of us are starting to look either further afield, or to places that are as unspoilt as Spain and Greece were 50 years ago. Overnight, it seems Turkey has become *the* place to go – and the time to go is *now*, while it is still relatively unspoilt.

But Turkey has had more than its fair share of bad press. Many people shy away from the idea of visiting the country, harbouring vague notions that it's unsafe, the people inhospitable and possibly dangerous, and the facilities primitive. Such notions are unfounded. Turkey is not altogether a paradise (where is?), but in many respects it beats the traditional competition hands-down.

Turkey is a very large country and, until quite recently, it was better suited to the traveller than the tourist. Almost everywhere roads have been improved, and while hotel facilities outside the major cities may not match the luxurious standards of their sophisticated Western counterparts, many are very comfortable, most are more than adequate, and almost all are spotlessly clean. In the major resorts there is every facility you would expect from other established holiday destinations, but with the added bonus of crystal clear, unpolluted sea, and service that is still, in the main, willing and enthusiastic.

Turkey is a unique mixture of Eastern and Western cultures, and a country extraordinarily rich and diverse in natural beauty. It is also a huge outdoor museum; scattered over its 780,000 sq km are the tangible remains of 10,000 years of history. It has played host to a dozen ancient kingdoms and empires, from the Bronze Age Hittites, through Classical Greece and Rome, to the Turkish Ottoman Empire. History is so intricately interwoven with myth and legend that it's sometimes hard to see the join. Here is Troy, where Greeks and Trojans fought for ten bloody years over Helen of 'the face that launched a thousand ships'; here too was the kingdom of Midas – he of the golden touch, and the route of Jason and the Argonauts in search of the Golden Fleece. Successive conquerors have everywhere left their mark: the boy-wonder, Alexander the Great, countless Roman emperors, including Antony and his Cleopatra, Tamerlane, the scourge of God, and a bevy of Seljuk and Ottoman sultans from Mehmet the Conqueror through to Abdul the Damned.

In the great city of Ephesus, in south-western Turkey, the Apostle Paul caused a riot preaching to the citizens; here too, St John wrote his Gospel, while keeping a protective eye on the Virgin Mary, who lived and died nearby, after the death of Christ. On the Mediterranean coast is the birthplace of St Nicholas, and the origin of the story that gave us Father Christmas. Indeed, all over this Moslem country there is evidence of the early days of Christianity.

It is not within the scope of this book to cover every single town, village and historical site in detail, but we have given information on all the major places of interest. With rare exceptions, we have avoided recommending specific hotels and restaurants; Turkey is developing rapidly, and a bad hotel or restaurant one year may be next year's 'wonderful find' or vice versa. But we have included a section on this subject which gives guidance on how to make the right choice.

A little knowledge of history and architecture helps to bring the ancient sites to life; so we have included a brief history of Turkey and an introduction to architecture. But if these things leave you cold, Turkey offers more hedonistic pursuits; wonderful beaches, excellent food, almost every kind of watersport and some of the best sailing waters in the world. Most facilities are as cheap, and mostly cheaper, than in the well-established European resorts.

Essentially Turkey has been written as much for the independent traveller as for those on a 'package', who want to make the most of their time in Turkey. If you are based in one resort, it will tell you which places can be visited from your base, and what to expect when you get there. For the independent traveller, the book is divided into logical, geographical areas, and each of the places included follows in sequence. We have started with Istanbul, undoubtedly one of the most fascinating cities in the world, and the key to the great diversity of cultures that have flowed back and forth across Turkey over the millennia.

It is a pitfall of many books of this type that they give you all the good news and little or nothing of the bad. There is no country in the world where there is perfection in everything, and an awareness of negative aspects can do a great deal to prevent disappointment. Therefore, where necessary, we have not pulled our punches.

Hittite lions

C·H·A·P·T·E·R · 1

Talking Turkey

The Turks

In the West, a fearsome image of the 'Terrible Turk' has been projected since the Middle Ages, when it was used to whip up crusading zeal to drive the Moslems from the Holy Land – a campaign in which the Christian 'liberators' were guilty of far greater barbarity than the Turks ever were. Much later the image was dragged out and paraded again, this time to justify the piecemeal distribution of the Turkish nation by the Allies after the First World War.

Now that Turkey has reasserted its nationhood and become a part of Europe, and now that 3 million tourists a year are flocking to holiday among the Turks, there has been a reappraisal of this fascinating people. So, who is the 'Terrible Turk'?

The Turks have been in Turkey for about 700 years. They were originally disparate tribes of nomadic warriors from Mongolia in Upper Asia. In the eleventh century, after years of isolated tribal incursions into Asia Minor, they arrived in force and settled on the Anatolian plateau.

The secret of their success lay in discipline, fearlessness, skilful horsemanship and an ability to move quickly, unencumbered by baggage or camp-followers. Each warrior had four horses, for meat, milk and riding. Meat was eaten raw, tenderised under the saddle as they rode. When the going was hard they would slit a vein in the neck of their horse and drink its blood.

They would breed with the women of whatever land they were passing through. The result is clearly apparent today. The Turks are a vigorous hybrid, with elements of Greek, Persian, Armenian, Georgian, Slav, Norman and Circassian – tall, blonde Circassian girls were shipped to the sultan's harem by the thousand. But there are many qualities and cultural characteristics common to all. The Turk obeys old laws and customs, long forgotten in the busy world of Western Europe; these are hospitality, generosity, care for the aged, sick and needy, a deep and universal love of children – and of animals – and a profound reverence for Islam.

Many Turks do have a rather fearsome and unsmiling countenance. But behind the façade is a warm, friendly and generous nature and a genuine desire to do everything they can to help you. Outside the established tourist resorts you will constantly be offered hospitality, and you may even find your bill paid in a restaurant, where a fellow Turkish diner will tell you that it is an honour to offer a meal to a stranger – and this from a people who can only dream of the sort of wages commonly earned in Western Europe!

The Turks are slow to anger – good manners and dignity restrain them far past the breaking point of most. But you will offend the Turk by taking in vain the name of Atatürk or by slandering Turkey or the Turks. This young nation was so bitterly fought for, the identity of its people so hard won, that these feelings should not be trifled with. 'Country First' (*Önce Vatan*) and 'Happy the man who can say "I am a Turk" ' (*Ne mutlu Türküm Diyene*) are two of Atatürk's famous slogans. In Ottoman times, 'Turk' meant 'Yokel' and was applied only to peasants; everyone who was anyone was an *Osmanli*. Today, the whole nation share in their heritage and all are proud to be called 'Turk'.

GEOGRAPHY

With the decline of the Ottomans, their empire gradually disappeared and by the time the Turkish Republic was founded in 1923, the borders of modern Turkey were clearly defined – all six of them. To the west, Turkey shares borders with Greece and Bulgaria, to the north-east, with Russia and to the south and east with Syria, Iraq and Iran; more than enough sensitive frontiers to keep Turkey's 630,000 man conscript army on its toes.

Turkey's land-mass covers some 780,000 sq km; although Turkey is described as being half in Europe and half in Asia, the former represents a mere 3 per cent of the total area. The Asian balance, known as Anatolia (*Anadolu*), takes the form of a high plateau, rising towards the east, where it culminates in the great mountains of Ararat and the Caucasus; at the edges, it falls away in steep mountain ranges, the Pontic chain in the north, and the Taurus to the south, to the surrounding seas.

This vast area offers virtually every type of scenery: arid plains, lush forests, dramatic mountains and peaceful lakes, and 8,000 km of varied coastline, from the steep, green hills of the Black Sea, to the rocky pine-fringed Aegean and the golden sweep of the Mediterranean sands.

Far from being a land of deserts, palm-trees and camels – a popular misconception – Turkey has a great deal of rich farmland, producing enough of a surplus to supply much of the Middle East, as well as exporting to Europe and elsewhere. The high plateaux have almost no rainfall, all the rain having fallen on the mountains behind the coasts, but they are irrigated by the waters of 15 rivers, including the Tigris, the Euphrates and the Maeander, as well as by a number of huge lakes, both natural and man-made, some as big as inland seas.

CLIMATE

Black Sea Coast A temperate zone, with high rainfall all year round, but mostly in autumn and winter; in spring and summer it may rain as much as once or twice a week. Summers are very warm, but not uncomfortable; winters are mild with frequent snow. (Swimming: June to September.)

Central Plateau A harsh land of extremes; in summer it's dry and baking hot – as you get higher towards the east, the nights, at least, are cool. In winter the cold is intense and travel is seriously hampered in the east by heavy snow. Spring and autumn are the best times for travelling here.

Mediterranean Very hot indeed in summer, and humid – even bananas grow here – with little or no rainfall. Winters are warm with moderate rainfall. (Swimming: May to October.)

Aegean Said to be the country's most agreeable climate; mild winters and hot summers, though not as excessive as the Mediterranean. Moderate rainfall in winter and spring. (Swimming: May to October.)

Istanbul The meeting point of all the continental and maritime climatic influences, Istanbul has hot summers with cool sea-breezes. The winter can be damp, cold and gloomy, with occasional snow. (Swimming: June to September.)

Average daily temperatures

	15 Jan °C	15 Jan °F	15 April °C	15 April °F
Istanbul	5	41	12	54
Izmir	9	48	16	61
Antalya	11	52	16	61
Ankara	7	45	12	54
Trabzon	0	32	11	52
Erzurum	−9	16	5	41

	15 July °C	15 July °F	15 Oct °C	15 Oct °F
Istanbul	23	73	16	61
Izmir	28	82	16	61
Antalya	28	82	20	68
Ankara	23	73	16	61
Trabzon	23	73	13	56
Erzurum	19	66	9	48

RELIGION

'There is but one God and Mohammed is His Prophet.' These are the words you will hear five times a day, chanted from minarets all over Turkey; it will, more than any other single experience, convince you that you are in Asia.

Some 98 per cent of the Turkish people are Moslem – followers of Islam – and, in spite of Atatürk's anti-Islamic reforms, the religion and its principles pervade every aspect of Turkish life.

The Moslem religion was born in Mecca in the sixth century. The Prophet Mohammed, who could neither read nor write, was said to have received revelations from God, which were collected into a holy book, known as the Koran – the base of the Islamic faith. Islam recognises earlier prophets and martyrs, such as Jesus and Moses, and even acknowledges the Bible as a holy work; indeed, Christians and Jews are honoured in Islam as 'People of the Book'. But, according to Islamic belief, the Koran is God's final, unadulterated word; everything that has been written before has been corrupted and distorted by man.

Islam is a simple faith, requiring five basic duties, the Pillars of Islam. The first duty is profession of the faith, requiring one to say, understand and believe that 'there is but one God and Mohammed is His Prophet'. Prayer, five times a day, is the second requirement, and must always be preceded by the ritual of ablution – washing of the hands, face and feet. The giving of alms by those who can afford it, is the third, and the fast of Ramazan and a pilgrimage to Mecca, the fourth and fifth.

Aside from teaching the good Moslem what he should believe, Islam also prescribes how he should behave. These moral guidelines are set down in a sacred code, known as *shari* and cover every possible eventuality. A good Moslem cannot separate his worship of God from everyday life, 'the mosque cannot be separated from the marketplace, nor politics from praise'.

Religious festivals

Ramazan Fasting is the fourth pillar of Moslem worship. During the daylight hours of Holy Month, Ramazan, a Moslem must abstain totally from any kind of food or drink. He must not even smoke (this must be particularly hard on the Turks for whom smoking is a national passion); Islamic festivals are celebrated according to the Moslem lunar calendar, eleven days shorter than the Gregorian calendar (in general use in Turkey and throughout the Western world). Consequently, Holy Month falls at a different time each year; it is particularly tough when Ramazan falls during the hottest part of the summer – understandably, tempers then can run a little high. Travellers, pregnant women, the sick and, of course, non-Moslems are excused the fast, and if you are based in a tourist resort you will hardly be aware of it. But in most of the cities, towns and rural areas, particularly in central Anatolia, the conservative heartland of Islam, many restaurants and cafes will not be open during the day. The fundamental reason for the fast is thanksgiving, and it is seen as an act of worship in which the mind is more than usually focused.

At dawn, drummers pass through the towns and villages, heralding the beginning of the day's fast. At sunset, the end of the fast is announced by the boom of a cannon. The shops, restaurants and tea-houses burst into busy life and queues form at the bakeries to buy the spicy flat Ramazan bread. Everywhere, Moslems can be seen hurrying home, parcels of food under their arms, for their lavish break fast meals. The 27th day of the fast is particularly significant. This is the day when the Koran was revealed by God to Mohammed. If you can

9

contrive to be invited into a Moslem home for this feast, you are in for a real treat. Traditionally the table is spread with an incredible array of food, representing the 'plenty of the earth'; spiced meats, olives, cheeses, honeycomb, thick cream and yoghourt, hot fresh Ramazan bread and all manner of vegetables and fruits. A family will often sit down to the table ten minutes or so before sunset and feast with their eyes until the cannon goes.

Şeker Bayram The festival of Şeker Bayram marks the end of Ramazan month; three days of rejoicing and gift giving, usually sweets or cakes. But the most important of the religious festivals is Kurban Bayram.

Kurban Bayram If you are in Turkey during the lead up to this holy day, you will notice sheep grazing in the most incongruous places. On the morning of Kurban Bayram itself, every household that can afford it will slaughter an animal, keeping some of the meat for themselves, but giving the greater part, including the skin and fleece, to the poor. This ritual is in commemoration of God's instruction to Abraham to sacrifice his son Isaac as a test of his faith. At the last minute, just before Abraham was about to slit his son's throat, God intervened, instructing him to substitute a ram. The whole business may seem a little barbaric to Westerners; but the animals are slaughtered more humanely than in any Western abattoir (Islam abhors unnecessary cruelty to animals) and hundreds of otherwise hungry people are well fed, at least for a few days. The festival itself lasts for three days and is the nearest equivalent to the Western Christmas. Banks and shops, except in the major tourist centres, are likely to be closed for the duration of Kurban Bayram.

ARCHITECTURE

Architecture is the one form of art to which nobody can be indifferent, for it is so inextricably entwined with our everyday life. In its basic form it is architecture that dictates whether or not you graze your knuckles on the door-jamb or crack your head on a low beam, or whether or not your food gets cold as it is brought from the kitchen to the table. In its more exalted forms it reaches the highest realms of sublime art. Between is the space in which we live.

Asia Minor is the finest outdoor museum of architecture in the world; it contains much of the best work produced by four major civilisations – Greek, Roman, Byzantine and Ottoman; to say nothing of the Hittites, Urartians, Armenians and Seljuks. However strong your inertia, your insistence upon lying in a stupor on a beach all day, you are eventually bound to be wheedled into visiting some ruins or remains, or even a building which is still standing. Even the smallest crumb of knowledge helps to guide the eye, concentrate the mind and make the experience far more enjoyable, so here are a few points:

Greek The architecture of the Greeks achieved a perfection of line, form and proportion rarely seen since. You need look no further than London or Paris to see how the laws formulated by the Greek mathematicians, physicists and architects are still the basis of all building design. Based upon mathematical formulae – the Golden Section, the Golden Triangle, etc. – the shapes are satisfying, and indisputably 'right', quite apart from their magnificence and beauty.

Left: Doric order. Right: Ionic order. Bottom: Corinthian capital

Greek temples depended largely for their effect upon the splendour of the setting: Zeus liked to be on mountains, while Poseidon preferred the head of a stormy cape.

The earliest school of Greek architecture was the DORIC ORDER, which evolved directly from the more primitive wooden buildings of around 1000 BC. The forerunner of the Doric temple would have been constructed entirely of wood, with a thatched roof. Later, the weight of the newly developed clay roofing tiles necessitated a stronger frame, and many of the conventions of building in wood were translated directly into stone – for instance the flutes of a Doric column resemble the work of a rounded adze, fashioning a log.

You can tell Doric architecture – of which there is not much in Asia Minor; most of it is in Greece – by its simplicity and a certain austerity of style. The columns are thick in proportion to the area they support; they are distinctly tapered, and rise directly from the base of the building; there are 20 flutes and the capitals are simple, shaped like a shallow casserole dish.

The IONIC ORDER, which is most of what you will see in Turkey, becomes more sophisticated, with slender, perpendicular columns, rising from moulded bases to 'Ram's horn' capitals; each has 24 flutes.

The final development, and the most flamboyant, is the CORINTHIAN ORDER. This is much like the Ionic, but has capitals decorated with 'acanthus leaf' sprays. The Romans liked and used the Corinthian in all their buildings.

The best place in Turkey to see pure Greek architecture, unadulterated by the Romans, is at PRIENE.

Roman The Romans were utterly absorbed by the Hellenic culture they inherited, particularly in architecture. They experimented with new materials, and added some important new forms, the ARCH and the VAULT, for ancient Greek architecture consists only of horizontals and perpendiculars; but the delicate beauty and perfection of the Greek buildings was never improved upon, and, under the Romans, tended to take on a somewhat heavy and utilitarian character. The Romans excelled chiefly in practical building, such as aqueducts, baths and cisterns. ASPENDOS and SIDE have some fine examples of Roman work.

Byzantine Greece, Rome, Christianity, and the influence of the Persians and Arabs, all merged into the art of Byzantium. The Pagan temples disappeared, and churches and monasteries sprang up in their place. The churches of Eastern Orthodox Christianity reflected the more transcendental outlook of their religious thought. The earlier Latin basilica-type churches focused the gaze of the congregation straight down the nave to the altar. The gaze and concentration of the Orthodox worshipper is directed upwards and outwards, into airy space, bounded by domes and vaults. In the development and perfection of this domed space lies the main achievement of Byzantine architecture. AGHIA SOFIA is the best example.

The other major achievement of Byzantine architecture is in the richness of the interior decorations. Paintings and, particularly, mosaics of religious subjects adorned the walls, vaults and domes of the churches, and were often used to mask unsightly structural necessities, such as the curious pieces known as 'squinches' and 'pendentives', which made the transition between the square, and the circular base of the dome.

During the years of ICONOCLASM (717–843), the building of churches almost died out, but when it returned, after the triumph of the ICONOPHILES, it blossomed in a different form. Churches were smaller, more intimate; they were built taller and narrower, with smaller domes, and with greater emphasis on exterior and interior decoration.

Ottoman The Ottomans continued the traditions of the Seljuks, Arabs, Persians and the Byzantines, and soon created their own highly original architecture. Aghia Sofia, the pearl in the crown of Byzantium, had fascinated them long before they took Constantinople; the influence it had on the development of their architecture is only too obvious.

For the Ottomans, as well as for the Byzantines, the hemispherical dome, set upon a square, represented the perfect symbol of earthly and heavenly space. One of the first Ottoman mosques is the FIRUZ AĞA CAMII in Istanbul; this is quite simply a square block with a dome and a portico. Later mosques emulated Aghia Sofia in the more complex use of space – the BLUE MOSQUE and the ŞEHZADE in Istanbul. In the eighteenth century, experiments were made with ideas from Europe, and a few Baroque-style mosques were built; but the idea never caught on, and the crowning glory of Ottoman classical architecture remained the sixteenth-century work of MIMAR SINAN.

Sinan was not only the greatest architect of the Ottoman empire, but is considered a major figure in world architecture. Born in Anatolia of Greek parents, in 1491, he was taken in the *Devşirme* to Istanbul, where he entered the Janissaries as a military engineer. He built bridges, barracks and arsenals, until his genius brought him to the notice of Süleyman the Magnificent. The two men became close friends – Sinan married Süleyman's daughter – and worked together to glorify the Imperial city. Over 300 buildings, the peak of Ottoman architecture, are attributed to Sinan. He died at the age of 97 – still building mosques.

Although there is great variety in the design of Ottoman mosques, there are a number of elements that remain constant; first there is the courtyard, often surrounded by a domed gallery, and with a *şardıvan* in the centre. As you enter the mosque by the main doorway (always covered by a leather curtain, to keep the coolness and silence in), you will see opposite, on the wall facing Mecca, the *mihrab*. This takes the form of a richly carved and decorated alcove, and serves metaphorically as a lens, to concentrate the prayer of the faithful upon Mecca. Near the *mihrab* is the *minber*, or pulpit, from which the Imam reads the sermon at noon prayer on Friday; the decoration on the *minber* is often extraordinarily ornate. There is no furniture, just deep carpets covering the whole floor. The main feature of a mosque is its space, and the grace and delicacy with which the great dome is supported and buttressed.

Glossary of Architectural Terms

AISLE The space in a church that runs parallel to, and beside the NAVE; usually separated from it by pillars.

APSE Recess at the east end of a church, behind the altar.

BASILICA The form of early Christian churches; a long NAVE, flanked by AISLES, leads to a semicircular APSE.

CAPITAL Crowning block of a column, upon which the roof rests.

CAVEA Seating area for the audience in a Greek or Roman theatre.

CORINTHIAN The last order of Ancient Greek architecture. Flamboyant, with 'acanthus' leaves.

DOME Hemispherical roof, widely used in Eastern Christian and Ottoman architecture.

DORIC Earliest Classical Greek order – austere, pure and simple.

FLUTE Vertical groove cut in a column.

HELLENISTIC Period from Alexander to Augustus – approximately the last three centuries BC.

IONIAN Middle order of Greek architecture – most of what you see in Turkey.

MEDRESE Religious school often attached to a mosque.

MIHRAB Pulpit of a mosque – often highly decorated.

MINARET Tower flanking a mosque, from which the prayers are called.

MINBER Elaborate niche in the wall of a mosque. It points the faithful towards Mecca.

NARTHEX Vestibule between the west door and the NAVE of a church.

NAVE The central space in a church, leading from the west door to the APSE.

ORCHESTRA Space at the foot of the CAVEA where the action takes place in a Greek theatre.

PROSCENIUM Raised stage on which the action takes place in a Roman theatre.

ŞADIRVAN Fountain, often elaborate, in the courtyard of a mosque, where ritual ablutions are performed before worship.

VAULT Arched structure of masonry, forming a roof.

Language

When the Turks were nomads tending their flocks on the steppes of Central Asia, their language was similar to the language spoken in Turkey today. This early Turkish was fine for discussing the weather or livestock; but as the Turks spread westwards, settling in new lands with new ideas and cultures, they found their language inadequate. There were no words for the business of administrating a settled community and nothing suitable for the religion of which they were soon to become the champions.

On the way to Asia Minor the Turks passed through the sophisticated worlds of the Arabs and Persians, becoming closely involved as slaves, mercenaries, and ultimately as high officials. As a result, the Persian and Arabic languages supplied the missing words.

Thus an Ottoman language developed, a curious hybrid, containing elements of all three languages, and squeezed uncomfortably into the Arabic script. The nobles and administrators could read and understand it; but it was quite unintelligible to the common people.

With the founding of the Republic, a priority was the reform of the language, so that the ordinary Turk could understand the affairs of government. Linguistic experts were put to work 'purifying' the language; sweeping out the Persian and Arabic words and replacing them with words of an original Turkic root. The Arabic script was exchanged for the Latin; this policy was implemented in an incredible six weeks! The result has been a spectacular rise in the rate of literacy: from 9 per cent in 1924, to over 75 per cent today.

Turkish is not an easy language; in the parts of Turkey visited by tourists, many people speak English or German, so you will have no trouble getting by; in the sticks, nobody speaks anything but Turkish, so it helps to learn a few words. The Turks will be delighted if you make the effort.

It is not within the scope of this book to give a comprehensive guide to the Turkish language; Berlitz do a handy phrase-book with a useful cassette; for a deeper understanding of the language, try *Teach Yourself Turkish* by Geoffrey Lewis or *Colloquial Turkish* by Yusuf Mardin. Here are a few simple phrases for everyday use:

PRONUNCIATION

Stress is more or less even on all the syllables of a word. All Turkish letters are pronounced as in English, but look out for the following:

a midway between 'but' and 'bat'
c like j in 'jam'
ç ch as in 'chop'
g always hard, as in 'give', never as in 'general'
ğ almost silent, perhaps a slight gurgle, or glottal stop. Lengthens preceding letter
ı short, like the first a in 'away'
j soft, as in French 'jeune'
o midway between 'hope' and 'hot'
ö as in German, a little rounder than the ur in 'hurt'
s soft as in 'this', never as in 'as'
ş sh, as in 'ship'
ü like French 'tu', not quite so much y as in 'tube'

Please	Lütfen
Thank you	Teşekkür ederim (at this point most people give up!)
Yes	Evet
No	Hayır
Good morning	Günaydın (literally 'Bright day')
Good afternoon	İyi Günler (Good days)
Good evening	İyi Akşamlar
Good night	İyi geceler
Hallo	Merhaba
Goodbye	Allahasmarladık (said by person leaving) or, alternatively, Güle güle

(literally 'Go laughing', said by person staying)

How are you	Nasılsınız
Excuse me	Affedersiniz
Today	Bugün
Tomorrow	Yarın
Yesterday	Dün
Turkey	Türkiye
England	Ingiltere
Holiday	Tatil
Work	Iş
Day	Gün
Week	Hafta
Month	Ay (also 'moon')
Year	Yıl
Beautiful	Güzel
Good	Iyi
Bad	Kötü
Big	Büyük
Small	Küçük
Hot	Sıcak
Cold	Soğuk
Old	Eski
New	Yeni
Open	Açık
Closed	Kapalı
Quick	Çabuk
Slow	Yavaş

Days of the week

Sunday	Pazar
Monday	Pazartesi
Tuesday	Salı
Wednesday	Çarşamba
Thursday	Perşembe
Friday	Cumar
Saturday	Cumartesi

Numbers

1	Bir
2	Iki
3	Üç
4	Dört
5	Beş
6	Altı
7	Yedi
8	Sekiz

9	Dokuz
10	On
20	Yermi
30	Otuz
40	Kırk
50	Elli
60	Altmış
70	Yetmiş
80	Seksen
90	Doksan
100	Yüz
1000	Bin

Numbers are built up in the most logical way possible; once you've learned the basic numbers above, just put them together (the hyphens are for clarification only).

16	On-altı
44	Kırk-dört
123	Yüz-yermi-üç
782	Yedi-yüz-seksen-iki
1986	Bin dokuz-yüz-seksen-altı

Useful phrases

I am English	Ingilizim
Do you speak English?	Ingilizce biliyor musunuz?
I don't understand	Anlamıyorum
Please could you speak more slowly?	Lütfen, daha yavaş konuşur musunuz?
I'm hungry	Acıktım
I'm thirsty	Susadım
I'm tired	Yorgunum
I'm lost	Kayboldum
Just a minute	Bir dakika
I'd like	Istiyorum
I don't want	Istemiyorum
A little more, please	Biraz daha, lütfen
How much is that?	Şu kaçadır? or Kaç Lira?
Where is the hotel?	Otel nerede?
Is there an empty room?	Boş oda varmı?
Do you have any wine?	Şarap varmı?
No!	YOK (accompanied by a raising of the eyebrows and a disdainful look down the nose; it's not supposed to be as offensive as it seems to an Englishman.)

Eating and drinking

There are, apparently, three great basic cuisines in the world; French, Chinese and... Turkish. You will be happy to believe this after your first meal in a fine Istanbul restaurant, and the same goes for many of the eateries in the tourist resorts and cities. Food in more remote eastern Turkey and rural areas can be rather uninspiring however. Nevertheless, if you enjoy good food, it is unlikely you will be disappointed in Turkey.

You will eat a great deal of lamb, the most popular of the meats, some chicken and beef, but no pork. Fish is plentiful in Istanbul and all down the coasts, although less so on the Black Sea. It is always a more expensive option than meat. Everywhere, there is a wide variety of excellent fresh vegetables – tomatoes, courgettes, peppers, artichokes, okra, pulses and aubergines, aubergines and more aubergines. Fruit and nuts are first class. Prices are universally low.

A typical breakfast will include crusty bread, occasionally toasted; sticky, sweet jam or honey; cheese – sometimes fresh, sharp sheep's cheese, but more frequently a tasteless processed triangle; a handful of black olives, slices of tomato and cucumber and perhaps a boiled egg. There are variations of course; some tourist hotels have given up on the olives! You can also ask for yoghourt; Turkish yoghourt, at its best, is the thickest and creamiest in the world; sweeten it with dollops of Turkish honey. You will almost always be given tea. If you ask for coffee you'll probably get a weak Nescafé. (Turkish coffee is a bit powerful first thing in the morning.) Expect to pay more for this; coffee is an outrageously expensive commodity in Turkey, and if you can't live without it, bring some with you and ask for hot water so you can make your own. You might get bacon in the big international hotels, but this is a Moslem country, so don't count on a British breakfast.

It's up to you whether you want to make lunch or dinner your main meal of the day but whatever you decide, there are plenty of restaurants, and snacks aren't a problem – street-food is a feature of Turkish life.

Generally speaking, Turkish restaurants can be divided into four categories. First there are the hotel restaurants. Leaving aside the big, luxury establishments, it's best to avoid eating anything but breakfast in a Turkish hotel. They usually attempt an approximation of 'international food' – whatever that is – and fail dismally. Added to this, they are frequently lacking in atmosphere. Don't book yourself into somewhere that insists on half-board; you really will be missing out.

The next two categories are loosely divided between

establishments calling themselves either *Restoran* or *Lokanta*. In practice, the use of the name is fairly interchangeable and arbitrary. In theory, *Restorans* display glass cases full of uncooked meat and fish, and a selection of *mezes*: salads, stuffed, pureed or chopped vegetable dishes, stuffed mussels, börek (flaky pastry filled with cheese, meat and sometimes spinach, served piping hot), yoghourt with cucumber or garlic (*cacik*), taramasalata and other savoury hors d'oeuvres. You choose a *meze*, or a selection, and then make your choice of meat or fish; this is cooked while you eat your starter. If you have room, you can usually order a syrupy dessert such as *baklava*; a Turkish version of creme caramel; or fruit in season. *Restorans* almost always serve wine, spirits and beer. *Lokantas* usually offer a selection of cooked dishes. You will be asked to make your choice, either from a display in the restaurant itself, or from the bubbling pots in the kitchen. There will be a soup (*çorba*), rice cooked in stock (*pilav*) and a variety of meat and vegetable stews. Many *lokantas* won't serve alcohol.

The specialist eateries make up the final category. The most popular of these is the *Kebapçi*. Inexpensive and fun, these places rarely sell alcohol. Here you will find all manner of kebaps; *çop kebap* is very small pieces of lamb cooked over a charcoal grill on little wooden skewers – you'll be given a great big bunch of them; *döner kebap*, slices of lamb carved off a revolving spit, *şiş kebap*, big pieces of lamb grilled over charcoal, *köfte kebap*, minced lamb, formed into meatballs and grilled on a skewer. All the kebaps will be served with great hunks of bread and a portion of salad. There are all sorts of regional variations on the kebap theme, and some are served with yoghourt or with a mildly spicy tomato sauce and hot butter. Look out for the *Pide Salonus*. Here you will find cheap, tasty Turkified pizzas; hot, flat doughy bread topped with a variety of goodies; the most popular is ground lamb with onions and tomatoes – a good bet for children, or for a quick, tasty, cheap snack.

There are several points to be aware of before eating out in Turkey. Don't judge a restaurant by its external, or internal decor. Before you go bonkers ordering a portion of every delicious *meze* in sight, ask what size the individual portions are; sometimes they can be quite large and you will be horrified when the waiter presents you with a groaning tray, just for starters. Turkish food is usually warm, *not* hot – this is not sloppiness on the part of the kitchen staff; the Turks like it that way. Service is often very quick, so if you want time between courses, it might be best to order your *mezes* and then go back to the counter to order your meat or fish. You can sit about after the meal for as long as the fancy takes you. If you have an unpleasant dish in one restaurant, don't necessarily dismiss it at the next. Many of the *mezes* look much the same, but are prepared in different ways. The yoghourt dish, *cacik*, for instance, is immensely variable and the quality of *börek* can range from crisp and delicious, to soggy and disgusting. Finally, don't feel embarrassed at the idea of walking into a restaurant, examining the food on display, and walking out if it doesn't appeal. After all, you check any other commodity before you buy; so why not food?

Turkey is a Moslem country, but you won't have any problem finding alcohol, especially in the tourist resorts. The most popular drink is *Rakı*. It's made from grapes and anis seed and known as *Aslan Sütü* (Lion's Milk). Beer is a popular drink and the two leading brands, available pretty well everywhere, are Tuborg and Efes Pilsen, both lager beers. Turkish wine is really quite good. You won't go far wrong with any wine labelled *Villa Doluca* or *Kavaklidere*; but as it's so cheap, you can afford to experiment. Spirits are a state monopoly and you can buy Turkish versions of whisky, gin, vodka and brandy. They are about half the price of imported spirits, but you may find them

Narghile, *or water pipe, and copper bowl*

difficult to acquire a taste for. If you buy Turkish brandy, buy the best; the cheap stuff is about as rough as you can get. There is a range of Turkish liqueurs, and these tend to be very sweet.

As far as soft drinks are concerned, you will find the ubiquitous Coca-Cola everywhere. Fruko is a fizzy orange drink and there is a good selection of fruit juices, although all are very sweet. You can buy flat or fizzy mineral water everywhere. *Ayran* is a traditional Turkish drink made with yoghourt, diluted with water and seasoned with salt. When it's good, it's very tart and refreshing, but the quality is variable. *Çay* (tea) is the national drink. It's served in small, glass cups which most Turks stuff with sugar. You might get a slice of lemon, but milk is unheard of. Turkish coffee has the sugar added while it's being brewed. If you just ask for Turkish coffee, you will probably be brought the *orta* version (medium sweet). You should ask for *sade* if you like it bitter, *az şekerli* if you want it sweetish or *çok şekerli* if your sweet tooth is beyond redemption. It comes in very small cups; don't drain it right to the bottom or you will get a mouthful of bitter grounds.

What to ask for

Whether eating or drinking out, or preparing your own meals, you will need to indicate what you want. Here are some useful words:

Anchovies	Hamsı	Apple	Elma
Apricot	Kayısı	Artichokes	Enginar
Aubergine	Patlıcan		
Banana	Muz	Beef	Sığıru
Beer	Bira	Bill	Hesap
Boiled	Haşlam	Break	Ekmek
Bream	Karagöz	Breakfast	Kahvaltı
Butter	Tereyağı		
Cabbage	Lahana	Carrots	Havuç
Cauliflower	Karnabahar	Caviar	Havyar
Cherries	Kıraz	Cheese (white)	Beyaz Peynir
Chicken	Piliç	Chocolate	Çikolata
Chips	Patates Kızartmısı	Chickpeas	Nohut
Coffee	Kahve	Cold	Soğuk
Courgette	Kabak	Crab	Yengeç
Cucumber	Hıyar		
Dessert	Tatlı	Dinner	Akşam Yemeği

Eggs	Yumurta		
Fish	Balık	Figs	Incır
Fork	Çatal	Fruit Juice	Meyva Suyu
Fried	Kızartmısı	Fruit	Meyva
Garlic	Sarmısak	Gin	Cin
Grapefruit	Greyfurut	Grapes	Üzüm
Green Beans	Fasulye	Grilled	Izgara
Hazelnuts	Fındık	Honey	Bal
Hot	Sıcak		
Ice Cream	Dondurma		
Jam	Reçel		
Knife	Bıçak		
Lamb	Kuzu	Lemon	Limon
Lemonade	Limonata	Lettuce	Marul
Liver	Ciğer	Lobster	Istakoz
Lunch	Öğle Yemeği		
Mackerel	Uskumru	Marrow	Kabak
Meat	Et	Melon – Yellow	Karun
Menu	Listesi	Milk	Süt
Mineral Water – still	Maden Suyu	Mineral Water – fizzy	Maden Sodası
Mullet – Red	Barbunya	Mussels	Midye
Mustard	Hardal		
Oil	Yağı	Okra	Bamya
Onion	Soğam	Orange	Portakal
Peach	Şeftalı	Pear	Armut
Pepper – condiment	Sıyah Biber	Pepper – vegetable	Biber
Pistachios	Şam Fistiği	Plaice	Pisi
Plate	Tabak	Portion	Porsyon
Radish	Turp	Rice	Pilav
Roast	Rosto		
Salad	Salata	Salt	Tüz

Sandwich	Sandviç	Sardines	Sardalya
Sea Bass	Levrek	Shrimp	Karides
Sole	Dil Balığı	Soup	Çorba
Spinach	Ispınak	Spoon	Kasık
Strawberries	Çilek	Stuffed	Dolma
Sugar	Şeker	Swordfish	Kılıç
Tea	Çay	Tomatoes	Domates
Tripe	Işkembe	Trout	Alabalık
Tuna	Palamut	Turkish	Lokum
Turkey	Hındı	Delight	
Yoghourt	Yoğurt		
Vegetables	Sebzeler	Vine Leaves	Yaprak
Walnut	Badem	Water	Su
Well-done (as of meat)	Iyi Pişmiş	Whisky	Viski
Wine – Red	Kırmızı Şarap	Wine – White	Beyaz Şarap

Shopping

Even if you don't plan to buy, you should visit a Turkish bazaar at least once during your stay; the best are in the big towns and cities. In the tourist towns, there is almost always a good selection of shops and if you avoid the stuff mass-produced for the tourist (thankfully, there isn't much of that yet) you may find a bargain.

Leather is good, and the leather clothes can be superb, though before you buy, try them on and check the quality of the workmanship – it varies. Copper and brassware are fashioned into every type of kitchen utensil, and the older items with their rich, dull gleam are particularly attractive, and reasonable. Costume and semi-precious jewellery is often of the chunky, unsubtle variety, but it can be very cheap. Gold and silver jewellery may be sold by the weight. Here too you can find good bargains, but look at the quality of the workmanship. Meerschaum pipes are sold everywhere; they can be intricately carved and are decorative in a 'Toby Jug' kind of way. You will find plenty of onyx, marble and alabaster, colourful handpainted ceramics, and richly embroidered shawls, headscarves and blouses. For edibles, try the boxes of Turkish Delight, pistachio nuts, herbs and spices – particularly cinnamon and saffron – all are worth finding space for.

But the star turn is indisputably the Turkish carpet. Every

Turkish kilim, *or prayer mat*

carpet salesman – and they are legion in Turkey – is convinced that you have come to Turkey for one thing only – to buy a carpet from him! Carpets and *Kilims* are more than a 'casual souvenir'. To buy something worth owning you will need to spend a considerable amount of money, but, if you are careful, you could be the owner of a work of art and an investment that could well outlive you.

The best carpets are woven in the villages, by women who have learned the tradition from their mothers; no artificial colours or dyes are used, the material is pure wool, cotton or silk. There are also machine-made carpets incorporating man-made fibres and artificial colours. How can you tell the real thing?

Fold the carpet double and look at the exposed roots of the pile; a hand-made carpet will be slightly irregular and the knots will resist the hardest tug. A factory-made carpet will display perfect lines of knots, quite straight; but if you pull hard on a tuft it will come out. Moisten a white handkerfchief and rub it over a patch; if the dyes are fast, your handkerchief will still be white, or just grubby. But if the colour is not good, it will come off on the handkerchief, and that means it will run or fade in the sun.

The finest and most expensive carpets are silk, made at HEREKE, near Istanbul. The best wool carpets come from YAHYALI near Kayseri, or are made by Kazakhs near Kars. The quality of the carpet is determined by the number of knots per square centimetre; the finest silk carpets are said to be knotted by the hands of children – as many as 200 knots per square centimetre.

Where do you buy? The first rule is to look in a number of shops before you commit yourself. You won't necessarily do better than in Istanbul and seeking remote villages to buy at source is a waste of time. When it comes to fine carpets, the carpetmakers rarely own the raw materials; the merchants have the whole operation arranged to benefit themselves.

If you are going to buy, you should haggle, but bear in mind that it's nothing more than a game. Every shopkeeper is aware that if you know nothing else about Turkey, and he'll assume you don't, you will know about haggling, and are bound to have a go; the price he originally quotes you will reflect this. Don't offer a silly price (i.e. less than 50 per cent of the original asking price). But you can start at about the 50 per cent mark and be prepared to move up by about 25 to 30 per cent. Don't haggle if you really don't want the item.

You are likely to be offered coffee or tea while you talk. Shopping in Turkey is an unhurried business, and for the shopkeepers it is an extension of their social lives. All day long they pop in and out of each other's shops, drinking endless cups of hot, sweet tea and smoking cigarettes. Don't feel guilty about accepting refreshment; it's not pressure to make you buy, but simply a way of life.

It is illegal to take antiques out of Turkey. At some of the classical sites you may be offered 'priceless antiques' by ragged children. The odds are the items will be worthless; but, don't risk taking them out – the penalties are high. The Turks are very sensitive about this as, over the years, their heritage has been systematically plundered by foreigners.

When buying a carpet, or any other expensive item, keep your receipt for presentation to Customs on leaving Turkey. This is very important.

Copper artefacts

HOTELS

If you are travelling independently, ignore the official listings and categories. The best way to find out if a hotel or *Pansiyon* is up to your particular standard, is to go in, look around and then ask to see the room. This isn't normal practice in Western countries, but it should be, and no one in Turkey will mind at all; don't hesitate to walk out if it's not up to scratch. Hotels and *Pansiyons* always display the prices of their rooms.

Accommodation is extremely varied. There are fancy hotels in Ankara and Izmir, including the big international chains in Istanbul. In all major towns, except in remote eastern Turkey, there is at least one hotel offering 'luxury' accommodation – i.e. rooms with en-suite baths or showers, roughly equivalent to a second-class Western hotel. Often a hotel with a dingy façade will turn out to be delightful inside (the reverse can also be true). You might expect a *Pansiyon* to offer less than a hotel; this is not always the case. Some of them, especially on the Aegean coast, are like small, modern hotels and are tremendous value for money.

You can pay anything from £1 (around $1.40) to £80 (around $110) for a bed for the night in Turkey. The minimum is usually roughing it. The other end of the scale is sanitised international splendour. In between there is something for everyone, and anything between £6 and £11 (around $8 and $15) a night can buy you a perfectly acceptable place to lay your head, even in a popular resort town.

TRANSPORT

Buses Everyone uses the bus system and this patronage has resulted in a truly exceptional service; comprehensive bus networks connect every city and major town. *Otogars* (bus-stations) are an experience in themselves; dusty, teeming with activity and incredibly noisy. There may be several bus companies plying the same route, competing with each other for your custom. There is no difference in ticket price, but there can be in the relative comfort of the bus itself, and the frequency of a particular service. You buy your tickets and reserve your seats at the ticket kiosks. You may be pounced on by a bus company hawker, who will take you to his company's ticket kiosk. Go with him, it won't cost you extra and he'll probably carry your bags; before you buy your ticket, ask what time the bus leaves. If you have to wait more than half an hour, check if another company has a bus that leaves earlier. If you have time to kill, most of the ticket kiosks will let you store your bags there.

The buses themselves are comfortable and clean, although for long journeys the seats are a bit hard. Every bus has a cassette machine. Jolly, Turkish music is the favourite, and if you travel a lot on the buses, you'll begin to think they all have the same tape – they probably do; it's repetitive but you can get a taste for it. At frequent intervals on long journeys, the *yardimci* will come round with a bottle of cologne. It's pleasant and refreshing. At the back of the bus is a cold box containing bottles or bags of cool mineral water. This is yours for the asking. The bus will make frequent stops along the way to allow you to get off to buy food and drink. As soon as the bus stops, snack vendors climb aboard selling all manner of goodies.

The bus system is cheap, efficient and fun; it's the best way of seeing the country and meeting the people.

Mini-buses Mini-buses work in much the same way as the buses, but serve shorter distances; again, they can be found in the *Otogar*. Destinations are displayed on a card inside the windscreen. Hang about by the bus; someone will approach you and let you know when it leaves. You may have to buy a ticket from a kiosk or pay the driver.

Taxis You will have no trouble finding taxis and, although they are expensive by Turkish standards, they are unlikely to break your budget. A lot of taxis now have meters, but check that it is working before you set off. If there isn't a meter, or if it's broken, agree a price before you leave. If there is a group of you, it's sometimes worth hiring a taxi for a private tour. Again, you should always agree a price before you leave. To give some idea of what to expect, a tour that would take the best part of a morning should cost the equivalent of about £20 ($30).

Dolmuşes *Dolmuş* literally means 'stuffed', and aside from being used to describe all manner of delicious vegetable dishes, it is one of the mainstays of Turkey's transport system. *Dolmuşes* are essentially shared taxis; they don't run to any specific schedule, but leave for their destinations when they are stuffed full of passengers – hence the name.

It can be a little difficult to cope with the *dolmuş* system but, if you can get to grips with it, you'll find it most helpful. In the big towns and cities, the *dolmuşes* ply specific routes; jump in and out of them at stopping places that are marked with signs saying *Dolmuş Indirme Bindirme Yeri*. The final destination of the *dolmuş* will be marked on a card in the windscreen.

In Istanbul and Bursa, many of the *dolmuşes* are wonderful old 'bath-tub' style American classic cars, with huge interiors, faded leather upholstery, and springs that have seen better days. Other *dolmuşes* look like taxis; so, if it's empty and you're not sure whether it is a *dolmuş*, ask before you get in. Often, on busy routes, mini-buses take over the *dolmuş* role.

By air If your time is limited and you need to get around quickly, try the Turkish internal airline system. It is remarkably cheap and there are airports all over Anatolia. All flights are operated by Turkish Airlines (*Türk Hava Yolları*); it is advisable to book.

By sea Turkish Maritime Lines have several services; all leave from Istanbul's Eminönü or Karaköy docks and cruise down the Black Sea, Aegean and Mediterranean coasts. They are very popular, especially the Istanbul-Izmir car ferry route, so you should always book in advance. Don't expect a luxury cruise ship – these boats are at best comfortably basic.

By train The services that connect Ankara, Istanbul and Izmir are all good and fast, offering daytime and night couchette services. The rest of the Turkish Railway network is generally very slow; it's a lot quicker by bus.

Car hire

Car hire is very expensive by Turkish standards but it is the best way of seeing the country; if there are four of you, it won't break the bank. In some respects car hire is preferable to taking your own car, as some of the sites can only be reached down very rough tracks, to which you might not care to subject your own car. All the big names in car hire are here and there is usually a local company as well. You need a driving licence and, although an international driving licence is not a condition of hire, it is better to have one. Most car hire companies take credit cards.

Driving Driving is on the right. Outside the cities, the roads are quite free of traffic and you won't see many cars, but you will encounter hundreds of big lorries, huge, intercity coaches and the occasional donkey, herd of goats or flock of sheep. Watch out for the sheep dogs; they regard your car as a menace and will run terrifyingly close to the wheels to chase you off. Avoid driving at night if you can; the headlights of oncoming traffic can leave something to be desired and there is no accounting for the nocturnal habits of goats and sheep.

The Turks are very horn-happy and it's as well if you adopt the same habit; give a blast on your horn on narrow roads as you approach a blind bend. Roads are generally good.

Yachting

Turkey has 8,000 km of coastline; nobody sails in the Black Sea, but the Aegean and Mediterranean coasts have some of the finest coastal sailing waters in the world. The sea is clean and perfectly clear; there are no tides to contend with; the wind is warm and predictable, and the coastal scenery is matchless. Flotilla sailing and bare-boat charters are very popular. Sailing in Turkey is not just the premise of the wealthy and you don't have to be an expert. Marina facilities are well-developed, particularly in Bodrum, Antalya, Kaş, Fethiye, Marmaris and Kuşadasi; but the real pleasure lies in the quiet anchorages where you can fish, swim or dive in perfect peace and isolation.

The coastline from Bodrum to Antalya is the area known as the 'Blue Cruise'. Boats can be chartered or hired from the port-towns down this coast. Shared between a group of you, this can be very reasonable when you take into account that it covers accommodation, travel and, sometimes, food – all rolled into one. If you plan to go in high season, you'll have to book in advance through a travel agent at home. But the best deals can be found by booking directly in Turkey at the port you wish to charter from.

ANNOYANCES

Plumbing At worst Turkish toilets, usually of the footplate variety, are unspeakable. The worst are found at the *Otogars* and to add insult to injury you have to pay a small amount to use them. Conserve the few coins you have for this purpose. Elsewhere the standard of cleanliness is quite reasonable, although Heath Robinson style plumbing makes each pull of the chain a novel and alarming experience. If you are planning to travel around, take your own loo paper.

Mosquitoes The problem isn't too bad, but if you are the kind mosquitoes like to eat, make sure you have repellent and invest in one of those little battery-operated machines that keep the little beasts at bay at night.

Noise Turkey is a noisy country. It probably won't bother you during the day, but if you want a good night's sleep check there isn't a minaret outside your hotel window. It is trying to be woken in the middle of the night and early in the morning by a tinny loudspeaker calling the faithful to prayer. During Ramazan the situation isn't helped by the noise of the drummers passing through the town, literally at the crack of dawn. Take earplugs.

Turkish drivers Everywhere in Turkey, the motor vehicle is King and pedestrians must fend for themselves as best they can. In Istanbul crossing the road can be a daunting experience. The best way to handle it is to fix your eyes firmly to the back of an Istanbulu and follow him doggedly and closely across, looking neither to the left nor right.

Carpet salesmen They can be annoyingly persistent but if they do lure you into their shop, ply you with tea or coffee and display every carpet they have at your feet, they are rarely offended if you leave without buying. If you don't worry, and you shouldn't, about the ethics or otherwise of wasting their time, these sessions can be instructive and a pleasant way to pass the time. Make it clear that you do not want to buy and sit back and enjoy yourself with a clear conscience. These salesmen often speak excellent English and are very knowledgeable about their own area.

C·H·A·P·T·E·R· 2

History

Çatal Höyük (6000 BC) is the world's oldest city after Jericho (8000 BC). Here in Central Anatolia were a peaceful, agricultural people. The mound of their city, near modern Konya, is 13 ha in extent; you can see the finds, simple pottery and sculptures of homely gods, in the Ankara Museum. This gentle civilisation seems to have been violently extinguished about 5000 BC.

Alaca Höyük and Kultepe are the sites of the next cast of characters, the Hatti; they too were a peaceful people with a veneration for the dead and a matriarchal society. They fell prey to the more energetic warrior Hittites, who arrived in 2000 BC. The Hittites enslaved the Hatti, and set about establishing a brilliant empire, moving south and east into Syria, where they clashed with the Egyptian Empire.

Symbol of the Hittite sun

GREEKS

About 1250 BC, Troy was sacked by the Achaeans, setting in motion waves of wandering tribes, heading east. Together with the 'Sea Peoples' and the Barbarians from the north and west, these 'Mixed Multitudes' brought the Hittite Empire to an end. Central Anatolia, organised and settled under the Hittites, reverted to primitive nomadism, for the new colonists preferred to stick to the coasts. Later, these coastal settlements were reinforced by an influx of Greeks, fleeing from overcrowding, oppression and the depredations of Barbarians in their lands to the west. The result was a brilliant flowering of Greek culture on the coasts, while the harsh steppes inland remained the domain of the Urartu, Phrygians and Lydians.

PERSIANS

In 540 BC, Cyrus, king of the Persian Empire, conquered the whole of Anatolia, reducing the coastal cities to the status of tribute-paying vassals. Persian rule was not irksome, though of course the tributes were unpopular, and a period of stability and prosperity followed, with the art and culture of the Greeks and Persians fruitfully intermingling.

ALEXANDER THE GREAT

In the space of eleven short years Alexander the Great changed the face of the known world. No other conqueror, either before or since, can match his precocious achievements.

He was born in 356 BC, the son of King Philip II of Macedonia. His father, a talented and energetic man, had spent much of his reign persuading other disparate and autonomous Greek states, either by argument or force, that united action needed to be taken against the Persians who had invaded Asia Minor and were in control of the Greek colonised city states on the coast. For their part, the Greek colonies weren't too bothered; Persian rule was, for the most part, just and they were left much to their own devices.

Head of Alexander the Great

Philip was assassinated before he could realise his ambitions but his son inherited both his throne, and his aspirations at the tender age of 20. Alexander had already built a considerable reputation as a general, cutting his teeth as leader of a series of successful campaigns while still only a 16-year-old, and summarily dealing with trouble from the Balkan tribes, to the north of Macedonia, who caused trouble immediately after the death of Philip.

Gathering his army, consisting mainly of highly-trained Macedonians, Alexander crossed the Hellespont (Dardanelles) in 334 BC, stopping midway to sacrifice a hapless bull to Poseidon and pour a golden cup of wine into the sea as a libation to the Gods. Approaching the shore of Asia Minor, Alexander resplendent in full armour, hurled his spear so that it landed 'true' in Persian dominated soil and leapt ashore ahead of his army. Alexander was a master of the dramatic effect.

His first encounter with the Persian army resulted in a decisive victory. Alexander then proceeded to 'liberate' the Greek city states. His reputation was already legendary and the cities, for the most part, adopted a prudent course of action and welcomed him with open arms and open treasuries. By 333 BC, after less than a year of fighting, Alexander was master of most of Asia Minor, his coffers were replenished and he moved on in hot pursuit of the Persians.

Coming face-to-face with the full might of the Persian army, led this time by the Great King of the Persian Empire, Darius III, Alexander was up against overwhelming odds. Yet again, he was victorious. Darius fled, the Greeks took control of the Persian camp and captured the king's mother, wife and daughters in the Battle of Issus near the modern town of Iskenderun.

Alexander didn't bother to pursue Darius. Instead he set his sights on Egypt and, progressing successfully through Palestine, he arrived in Egypt where he was greeted with hardly a whisper of resistance. For a while Alexander busied himself with reorganising Egyptian administration and founding the great city of Alexandria. On a whim, he visited the famous Shrine of The God Ammon, in what is now the Libyan desert. Here the oracle hailed him as 'Son of Ammon'. This was all Alexander needed to convince himself that he was a god. The rest of the civilised world didn't need much persuading; with the exception of Darius. Once again, Darius had gathered a huge army and Alexander returned to Asia Minor and battle with the Persian king. Once again, Alexander was victorious; this time, decisively.

Now Alexander, a mere 29-year-old, was master of the greater part of the civilised world. In general his rule was wise and just. He treated the conquered with honour and respect and made a point of adopting the religious practices of whatever country he happened to be in at the time. He had a vision of a fusion of the peoples of Greece and of the Persian Empire. To this end, he ordered 10,000 of his officers and troops to marry local Persian women and offered a dowry to each couple, himself setting an example by espousing the late King Darius's daughter, Statira. It must have been the biggest, and most expensive, wedding party in the history of the world.

In 327 BC Alexander turned his attention to India. His army advanced for months and months, through hitherto uncharted territory, as far as the River Ganges. Here, Alexander met with the first, and only, real resistance in his entire career; and it came from his own army. Exhausted and further from home than they had ever believed possible, the soldiers dug in their heels and refused to budge. Furious, but impotent, Alexander was forced to turn back.

Alexander died shortly afterwards, in Babylon, on 10 June 323 BC; not in glorious battle, nor by the assassins' knife, but rather prosaically of the fever. Had he lived he might well have had the chance to carry out his dream of a world empire with Europeans and Asiatics fused into one race, and the history of the world would have been very different.

Understandably, Alexander had not envisaged such a shortlived career and had made no provision for his succession. He left behind only an idiot half-brother and an unborn son. His vast empire was thus, by default, divided arbitrarily amongst three of his generals; Antigonus, Lysimachus and Seleucus who at first agreed their individual spheres of influence and then immediately proceeded to fight each other for over a generation.

ROMANS

The rising empire of the Romans flooded over all that was Greek in the Mediterranean and Asia, becoming Hellenised itself in the process. The Seleucids, the last of the dynasties left by Alexander's generals, were defeated at Magnesia in 190 BC. Roman rule, the 'Pax Romana', brought peace and stability to Anatolia for over three centuries; this period saw the building of the great Roman cities of the 'Province of Asia'. With its rich resources and established culture, Anatolia became an important part of the Roman Empire, so when the huge unwieldy empire split into east and west in 330 AD, the natural site for the eastern capital was Byzantium, at this time known as Constantinople. At the same time, the Emperor Constantine declared Christianity the official religion of Rome.

BYZANTIUM

As Rome in the west collapsed under the onslaught of the Barbarians, the 'New Rome' of the east became the Byzantine Empire, which, as the bastion of Christianity against the tide of Islam, would continue to hold the power at Constantinople for 1,000 years.

The empire reached its territorial and cultural zenith under

Justinian (527–65). Justinian built the great symbol of Byzantine glory, Aghia Sofia; he also extended the borders to include southern Spain, North Africa, Egypt, the Middle East, Anatolia, the Balkans, Greece and Italy. Worship of the old pagan gods had been forbidden in 380; now Christianity was enforced throughout the empire. The emperor himself was the representative of God on earth; Byzantium became known as the 'Empire of Warriors and Monks'.

But the empire had over-reached itself, and Justinian's successors were not strong enough to hold it together. The long process that would finally decimate the empire, had started. The frontiers were under constant attack; famine and pestilence, religious dissent, and successionary strife weakened the empire from within. In 1071, the might of the Byzantine army was routed in Anatolia by the newly arrived Seljuk Turks; from now on, the old order was doomed.

In 1204 a fatal blow was struck when the Latin Christians of the Fourth Crusade sacked Constantinople. The emperor fled from the carnage to Nicaea (now Iznik), where the embers of empire glowed for a few years more. In 1261, with the aid of an army of Turks, the old order re-took the Great City. A brief and glorious renaissance of art and culture followed, but it was not to last.

The Prophet Mohammed had prophesied that one day the Great City would fall to Islam, and it had long been the aim of every Moslem leader, Arab or Turk, to take Constantinople. The city had often been attacked and besieged, but never by anyone of the calibre of Mehmet II and the Turks of the tribe of Osman. In 1453, after one of the most gallant defences in history, Constantinople fell. The Emperor Constantine XI died wielding a sword, and the Empire of Byzantium was finished.

THE OTTOMAN EMPIRE

The Turks came in waves from the steppes of north-east Asia. The first to arrive in Anatolia were the Seljuks, making their presence felt by thrashing the Byzantine army at Manzikert in 1071. Eventually they settled at Konya, where they established a civilisation glorious in culture, art and Islamic scholarship. In order to secure their frontiers, under constant threat from the Byzantines, the Crusaders, Karamanians and Mongols, they had a policy of settling warrior tribes, *Ghazis*, on the disputed marches.

One of these warrior tribes, under the leadership of Osman, would establish the dynasty that was to dominate Islam and scourge Christianity for over three centuries – the *Osmanli*, or

Mehmet II, the Conqueror

Ottomans. The *Osmanli* were exceptional; brilliant warriors though they were, it was their organisational ability and statesmanship that won for them the prizes which eluded other tribes.

By 1390, the Ottomans, with their capital now at Bursa, had made large gains in Anatolia, the Balkans and Greece, at the expense of the Byzantines. Mehmet II extended the territories still further, and earned the acclaim of all Islam by taking Constantinople. In 1453, after an extraordinary siege, the Great City of Christianity became the seat of the Ottoman Empire. Mehmet, now known as the 'Conqueror', set about building an Imperial city fit for the sultans. He called it Istanbul.

The Ottoman Empire enjoyed its glorious age under Süleyman the Magnificent (1520–66). By now, Hungary, most of North Africa and Egypt were part of the empire. Istanbul became the most sophisticated city in the world, adorned with majestic monuments and steeped in all the luxuries provided by a far-flung empire. People of many nations walked the streets in freedom and security, free to worship as they pleased. Süleyman was known as the 'Lawgiver' to his own people, for he codified the laws, and established as just and liberal a society as the age permitted. The common people of the conquered nations often saw the Ottomans as deliverers rather than conquerors.

But although Süleyman was perhaps the greatest of the Ottoman sultans, it was he who sowed the seeds of decline. The lascivious opulence with which the sultans were surrounded, was to take its toll. Previously the sultan would ride out to war every summer at the head of his armies. The harshness of military life was an antidote to the stultifying influence of the court. Süleyman had showed himself a matchless soldier in many campaigns, but as he grew older, he preferred to stay at home, leaving the conduct of campaigns to his viziers. He was the last sultan to ride out to war.

Süleyman moved his harem to the palace, next to the *Divan*, the seat of government. From now the pernicious eunuchs and pampered women of the harem were to play a central role in the decline of the empire. Süleyman also granted the first of the 'Capitulations', the trading and territorial concessions given to the French, Dutch, British and Russians. As a result of these concessions, the European nations became a law unto themselves within the Ottoman Empire, an implacable enemy presiding over its downfall.

Süleyman was succeeded by his son, Selim – the 'Sot'. Now we see the sobriquets of the earlier sultans – Conqueror, Thunderbolt, Formidable, Magnificent – give way to less flattering epithets: Sot, Drunkard, Mad, Damned, etc. Selim and later sultans were too feeble to control the great machines that had hitherto constituted the strength of the empire. One of the bastions of the empire had been the 'Janissaries'; this elite fighting force, the spearhead of the Ottoman army, consisted of selected conscripts from the sons of Christian subjects, taken into the Islamic faith and given the most rigorous training (the *devşirme*). Now they were to turn against their masters, deposing and assassinating sultans, dictating military policy and generally disrupting the affairs of empire. Reversals followed throughout the Ottoman territories and, by the middle of the nineteenth century, the Ottoman Empire had been whittled away to the bare bones of Anatolia and Thrace.

Russia, eager for control of the Bosphorus and the Dardanelles, now engaged in almost continuous war with the Ottomans. The Europeans, more fearful of the Russians, reversed their anti-Ottoman policies and rushed to support the tottering empire.

There were still a few sultans who boldly attempted reform. Selim III instigated political, economic and military reforms. Mahmut II established a new army, trained on European lines; with these troops he massacred the Janissaries in 1826, an event known as the 'Auspicious Incident'. But the best efforts of the reformers could do little to delay the inevitable.

Abdul Hamid reigned, as the last of the real Ottoman sultans, over an empire dubbed the 'Sick Man of Europe'. Though the rot permeated the whole empire, it came from the top. Voices of dissent started to call for an end to the absolute power of the sultan, particularly among the military and the young who had been educated abroad. By 1876 the underground movement, the 'Young Turks', had gained enough ground to force Abdul Hamid to proclaim a constitution. This he did reluctantly, but almost immediately revoked it and resumed absolute control, murdering Midhat Paşa, the leading figure among the reformers.

But by 1908 the Young Turks were powerful enough to re-impose the constitution, depose Abdul Hamid, and, as the Committee for Union and Progress, take the reins of power. The CUP ruled harshly and absolutely, permitting no dissent, instigating the atrocious massacre of the Armenians, and generally making a bad situation worse.

Turkey was seduced by the Kaiser into entering the First World War on Germany's side. When the war was lost, it was the Allies' piecemeal annexation of Turkey which pushed the Turks into a corner and caused them to gather the threads of national pride and rally to the flag of Atatürk. Thus was born the Republic of Turkey.

MUSTAFA KEMAL ATATÜRK

If you didn't know who Mustafa Kemal Atatürk was before you visited Turkey, you certainly would by the time you came back. His photograph, portrait or statue is everywhere. The smallest village boasts a statue in the square, every shop will display at least one photograph and you won't pass through a hotel reception without encountering his stern gaze. If you're still in any doubt as to the position this extraordinary man holds in the majority of Turkish hearts, a visit to his mausoleum in Ankara will convince you. It is one of the most outstanding modern monuments ever built to the memory of one man.

Atatürk, the 'Father of Modern Turkey', was born in 1881, in Macedonia; a birthplace shared with Alexander the Great. The son of lower middle-class parents, he embarked early on a military career.

Mustafa Kemal Atatürk

The years before the outbreak of the First World War saw the first stirrings of discontent amongst the people, especially the young, against the decadence of the Ottoman Sultanate. Atatürk was active in the 'Young Turk' movement which proclaimed a constitution, stripping the sultan of much of his power. Atatürk was never given a position of authority in the movement. Hot-headed and outspoken, he made many enemies among his contemporaries and was effectively banished to the political wilderness. But, as a soldier, he started to build a formidable reputation. In the battle of Gallipoli, fought against the Allies in the First World War, he was the only commander to assess the situation realistically and heroically led his troops to victory.

By the end of the war, Turkey was thoroughly defeated; the Allies were poised to carve up what was left of the Ottoman Empire among themselves. Russia, France, Britain and Italy all had their eyes on Turkish lands. The Turkish government was so enfeebled and the sultan so abject and ineffectual that there was little resistance to the humiliating treaties legalising the dismembering, not just of the remains of the Ottoman Empire, but of Turkey itself. Indeed, the situation might well have continued that way, had it not been for the 'joker in the pack' – Greece. In 1917 the British had dangled the carrot of 'large concessions on the coast of Asia Minor' under the Greek nose, as an inducement to their entry into the war. Greece needed nothing more by way of encouragement, as she had long harboured territorial ambitions in that direction. When the war was over the Greeks started to clamour for more territory, namely *all* of the Aegean coast of Asia Minor and inland. In spite of opposition from the other Allies, Britain actively encouraged the Greek claims, and eventually a force of 20,000 men occupied Smyrna (now Izmir).

Turkey was defeated, humiliated and its spirit all but extinguished. It was clear that if the future of the country was left in the hands of the sultan and his government, there would *be* no Turkey at the end of the day.

Atatürk's moment had arrived. Slipping quietly out of British-held Istanbul he made for Ankara and from there began, against enormous odds, to raise the listless populace to action.

The Greek occupation of Smyrna was just the catalyst that was needed, and Atatürk's Nationalist movement suddenly gained momentum as hundreds of Turks stealthily made their way to Ankara to rally to the cause. Thus began the Turkish War of Independence, which lasted for two years until 1922, and succeeded in driving back the Greek forces, eventually expelling them from Turkish soil. Above all, it succeeded in giving back to the Turks their self-respect and confidence; they owed it all to one man – Mustafa Kemal Atatürk.

In the 16 years that followed the war, Atatürk as President of the new Turkish Republic, brought about a total transformation of his country. Turkey is essentially a country with an eastern culture, religion and values. Atatürk was convinced that the only way forward was Westernisation and he set about introducing reforms to this end.

The most difficult barrier to reform was the reactionary stranglehold of Islam. Since childhood, Atatürk had developed a strong dislike of many of the practices of Islam; his first goal was to reduce the power of the religious leaders. The Turks were governed by Islamic law; religious courts dealt with all matters whether civil, commercial or criminal. Atatürk disman-tled the religious courts and replaced them with an exact replica of the Swiss Legal Code, lock, stock and barrel. He banned the studying of the Koran in schools and outlawed a number of fanatical Islamic sects. Civil marriage ceremonies were made compulsory.

In 1925 he passed the famous 'Hat Law' which outlawed the wearing of the Turkish fez. Atatürk had always loathed the fez, having once been made fun of during a trip overseas. There was a great deal of initial resistance to the new law. The fez had a symbolic as well as a religious significance and some eastern provinces were incited to riot over the ban. But eventually, the Turks buckled down and the hatters of Europe had a field day, offloading tons of inappropriate and outmoded headgear onto the hat-hungry Turkish public.

In 1934 Atatürk gave women the vote and attempted to speed their emancipation by outlawing the wearing of the *yashmak*. A story is told of Atatürk's ruse to ensure the law was obeyed; sometime after the veil was abolished, a further order was published to the effect that all prostitutes *had* to wear the veil. The following day not a *yashmak* was to be seen on the streets of Istanbul. But in the long term, this measure was less successful than Atatürk's other reforms. Certainly in the more sophisticated cities and towns the law had some effect, but in the countryside and in the more conservative cities the veil was still worn, as it is in many places today.

Next, Atatürk turned his attention to the language. Turkish was heavily influenced by Arabic and Persian and had developed into an unwieldy and immensely complicated hybrid, with the written word becoming almost the sole premise of the educated classes. The rest of Turkey was illiterate and was likely to stay that way, unless measures were taken towards simplification. Not only did Atatürk replace the flowery Arabic alphabet with Latin-based characters, but he rooted out many of the Arabic and Persian words and replaced them with new words based on an original Turkic root. He insisted, with characteristic impatience, that the language be 'installed' within six weeks, and to show that he really meant business he himself went out into the parks and the streets to teach the people.

The changes came thick and fast. Now the people were directed to adopt a surname. Hitherto they had been known as *'Mustafa son of Ahmed'*, or suchlike; a confusing and outmoded state of affairs. The traditional day of rest had always been the Moslem holy day, Friday. To bring Turkey into line with the rest of the Western world, Sunday was now declared the day of rest and so the 'weekend' was introduced to Turkey.

Atatürk died on 10 November 1938 in the Dolmabahçe Palace in Istanbul. Less than 20 years previously, Turkey had been a country with no future, struggling hopelessly under a medieval and totally outmoded political system, with a people who had lost their confidence, self-respect and sense of direction. In the short time allotted to him, Atatürk turned the tide and presided over the new nation that is today's Turkey.

Turkey since Atatürk

Atatürk's Republican People's Party was the only political party after the establishment of the republic. By 1950 though, it was considered safe and appropriate to permit the existence of a political rival, the Democratic Party. In the elections of 1950, the Democratic Party, under Adnan Menderes, swept the board. They continued to hold power for ten years, governing ineffectually, destroying the economy and discouraging all opposition. In 1960 the army, in its unusual role as a supporter, rather than a subverter of democracy, stepped in and took control. The corrupt leaders of the government were tried and imprisoned; Menderes was executed.

In 1961, a new constitution was adopted by popular referendum. General elections in 1965 returned the Justice Party, very similar in complexion to the Democratic Party. The army took a pace back and watched. Towards the end of the 1960s, Turkey erupted with civil unrest; extremists of both right and left battled in the streets, and the population, caught in the crossfire, became restive. In 1971, the army stepped in to put the government back on what they thought was the right lines.

Elections held in 1973 and 1977 succeeded only in putting weak coalitions in power. By 1980, strife between opposing extremist factions almost led to civil war. Again the army intervened. General Evren, the leader of the army, whose picture nowadays you sometimes see beside Atatürk's, won enormous popularity by this action. He was subsequently voted in as president. Turgut Ozal, the current Prime Minister, continues to work a ponderous way towards full democracy – and Europe.

C·H·A·P·T·E·R·3

Istanbul

P<small>AST</small>

Some 3,000 years ago, there was a fishing village on the headland between the mouth of the Golden Horn and the Sea of Marmara. A perfect site for a village, it was blessed with cool sea-breezes in the heat of summer, while the hill protected the anchorage from storms. The land was fertile, and the straits, rivers and seas teemed with fish.

In 700 BC, a band of land-hungry Greek colonists chanced upon this idyllic spot. Legend has it that their chief, Byzas, consulted the Oracle at Delphi, and was advised to land 'opposite the blind'. The meaning of this curious advice became clear as he entered the strait. On the Asian shore, another group of colonists had already settled at Chalcedon – today's Kadiköy – and certainly they must have been blind to miss the infinitely preferable site across the straits. Accordingly Byzas

Traditional ornamented shoe-shine box

landed, walled off the tip of the headland, and – with the assistance of Apollo and Poseidon – set about building a town. He called it BYZANTIUM.

The town survived and flourished under the Greeks, Persians and Romans, until, in 191 AD, it cast its lot with the loser in a Roman civil war. Septimius Severus, the victor, demolished the town and put most of the inhabitants to the sword. Soon afterwards though, seeing the potential of the city, he thought better of his hasty action, and rebuilt and extended it in much grander style, naming it AUGUSTA ANTONINA, after his son.

In 330 AD, as the Roman Empire expanded and split into east and west, the Emperor Constantine declared Augusta Antonina the capital of the eastern Roman Empire, the New Rome. He called the great city CONSTANTINOPLE.

During the next 1,000 years, Constantinople became one of the greatest and most powerful cities on earth. It was the heart of the Byzantine Empire, the head of the Eastern Christian Church and the centre of immense military power, and cultural and mercantile wealth. From the reign of Constantine it conquered and grew, reaching its zenith during the rule of Justinian in the sixth century. But, by the beginning of the fifteenth century, it was a pale shadow of its former glory, weakened by internal dissent and ceaseless battering from surrounding Turks and Barbarians, and the Crusaders of the Latin Church. In 1453 the Great City fell to Mehmet the Conqueror, Sultan of the powerful *Osmanli* dynasty – the Ottomans.

ISTANBUL was the name the Ottomans gave to their new

Elaborate balcony of an Istanbul minaret

capital – (from Greek εις την πολην = in the City). Mohammed the Prophet had prophesied long ago that the forces of Islam would one day take the Great City, so Mehmet, who had finally realised the dream of every Moslem, set about turning it into a fitting capital for the Islamic world. As the empire of the Ottomans grew, immense wealth was channelled into the coffers of the city. The finest architects, builders, artists and craftsmen were gathered from all over the empire to glorify Islam and the magnificent capital of the Sultanate.

Under Süleyman the Magnificent, Istanbul and the Ottoman Empire achieved their zenith; from this period, dates most of the best Ottoman architecture of Istanbul. But with the death of Süleyman and the accession of his son Selim (the Sot), the Ottoman Empire started its slow decline until, under the wretched Abdul Hamid (the Damned), the Sultanate was abolished altogether. In 1923, Atatürk moved the capital of the new Republic of Turkey to ANKARA, partly because of the old Great City's associations with the backwardness and venality of the last Ottomans, and partly, perhaps, metaphorically to pull the Asian side of the new nation into twentieth-century Europe.

PRESENT

When the seat of government moved to Ankara 60 years ago, Istanbul was pensioned off as the capital. But in spite of this, Istanbul, with its incomparable location, its monuments, its style and grace and its indomitable life, remains the spiritual capital and a vital symbol of Turkey past and present.

'The Great City' as Istanbul or Constantinople has long been known, straddles seven hills at the mouth of the BOSPHORUS, the forest-lined ribbon of water that joins the Black Sea to the Sea of Marmara, and divides Continental Europe from Asia. Flowing through the heart of the city is the GOLDEN HORN, a wide river rising 11 km inland, in the eastern hills of Thrace. Today the city has one foot in Europe and one foot in Asia, reached by a short ferry-trip, or a drive over the new Bosphorus Bridge.

The first thing you notice is the water; there is water everywhere, a river, a strait and a sea that are the main thoroughfares and an intrinsic part of the life of the city. From the palaces, mosques and towers that crown the hills, shady narrow streets drop straight to the water's edge. Lining the Bosphorus, glorying in their own reflection, are more palaces and mosques with marble quays or deep, rocky harbours. The sea is part of the city and its life, as in Hong Kong or Venice.

Eminönü

Eminönü is the heart of the city's waters and as good a place as any to begin a tour of Istanbul. Here, at the point where the Golden Horn flows into the Bosphorus, are the STEAMER TERMINALS, the *Eminönü Iskele*. It's like a bus-station for boats; at any time of day there are dozens of steamers to take you anywhere in the city, either to the European or the Asian side, north to the Black Sea or south to the Sea of Marmara. This is the best way to see Istanbul; it's as cheap as the buses, almost as regular, more comfortable and much more fun.

Should you be hungry, this is also one of the best places to eat. Sit at one of the fish restaurants under the GALATA BRIDGE: this bridge, the artery betwen Old Istanbul (Stamboul) and BEYOĞLU, floats on pontoons and is moved aside every morning to allow shipping to pass in and out of the Golden Horn. There have always been fish restaurants beneath the bridge; they used to be simple and cheap, but the spot has become so popular with tourists, that they have all moved up-market. The quality is excellent, but this is no longer a cheap place to eat – pleasant though, sitting virtually on the water beside the steamer quays.

For cheaper fare, follow the example of the Istanbulus and buy your food from a street-hawker on the quay. The best of all is fresh fish, cooked before your eyes and stuffed in a bun with some salad. You can spend an agreeable hour watching the astonishing spectacle provided by the team of fishermen/chefs; the team consists of a loaf-cutter, a fish-gutter, a placer of prepared fish in the enormous pan of boiling oil, a remover of the cooked fish, a stoker who keeps the fire going and replenishes the oil in the pan, and a treasurer who assembles the bun, fish, tomatoes and onions and takes the money. The whole process is carried on at great speed, from a wildly pitching rowing-boat, hurled about by the wash of the departing steamers.

On the quay itself you can eat giant mussels, charcoal-grilled; corn-on-the-cob, pizzas, *lahmacun*, salads, *simit*, enormous peaches from Bursa, nuts from the Black Sea – and to drink: *limonata, ayran, vişne*, apricot-juice or iced water. This is one of the gastronomic highlights of Istanbul.

Yeni Valide Camii

Cross the footbridge over the road, and you come to the towering Yeni Valide Camii. Built between 1597 and 1663, it was commissioned by Valide Sultan Safiye, the mother of

Mehmet III. This mosque is richly decorated with tiles, and is noted for the beauty of its *şadırvan*. Sheltering under the walls of the mosque is a busy market, which illustrates well the inseparability of Islam from everyday life and commerce. It's not one of the 'Great Mosques' of Istanbul, but its situation at the hub of the market on the waterfront, its fine tilework, and the beautiful arched galleries on the steps – and a rather fine gateway on the north-east side – make it very pleasing.

Beside this mosque is the MISIR ÇARŞISI – the EGYPTIAN MARKET. When Egypt fell to the Ottomans in the sixteenth century, caravans and shiploads of exotic goods, hitherto unknown in Istanbul, began to arrive in the city; the Egyptian Market was built to house this trade. Like most of the secular buildings of the city, it was constructed of wood; and in common with most of these buildings, it caught fire frequently, until in 1609 it was razed to the ground. This time it was rebuilt in stone, and the traders returned to continue the sale of mastic and antimony, roots, seeds and dyes, henna, sandalwood and gum. In the rooms over the gate sat the Commercial Court, where a team of judges would check weights and measures, and see that no merchant cornered the market in any particular commodity. Today, in these rooms, you can eat some of Istanbul's best food at PANDELI'S RESTAURANT – up the steps by the gate (only open at lunchtime). Today, the market sells the mundane household necessities of everyday life, but it still offers herbs and spices, and is heady with their scents and strident colours. Here too, you will find stalls devoted to Turkish sweetmeats, slabs of Turkish Delight, quite different from the commercial rubbish that masquerades under the same name. There are vats of honey from which you will be invited to taste the different varieties. There are stalls selling unguents and ointments, pills and petals, and the dried lizards and toads, so unaccountably popular in the Orient. The biggest seller is the mysterious 'Aphrodisiaque des Sultans'. Nobody will tell you anything about this promisingly named substance until you've bought it.

Between the Egyptian Market and the Yeni Camii is a shady park with a tea-garden; here you will find the city's nursery and seedsmen's market, where you can buy seeds and bulbs, jasmine, geraniums, fruit-trees, palms and humble pot-plants. A section of the market is devoted to an Oriental version of 'pets' corner'; for sale are songbirds, whose voices fill the garden, terrapins, rabbits, snakes, mice, chickens and ducks and jars full of beasties that look suspiciously like leeches. This is one of the mercifully cool and quiet corners of the city.

In Eminönü too, is the main CITY BUS-STATION, for regular

buses to all parts of the city and up and down the Bosphorus. You buy a book of tickets from a booth, or pay a few lira more to buy it from a hawker, who makes an officially sanctioned living by this method – though, quite obviously, not a luxurious one. When you enter a bus, slip the ticket into the metal box by the driver, and you're on for as far as you wish to go.

Just to the east of Eminönü Quay is Istanbul's EUROPEAN RAILWAY STATION, SIRKECI. Follow the road in front of the station, ANKARA CADDESI, and keep going up the hill; this takes you to the centre of the old city, SULTANAHMET, where most of the main monuments are to be found.

AGHIA SOFIA

You can't miss the church of Aghia Sofia; it crowns the city from the hill of Sultanahmet, and is one of the largest and most important religious monuments in the world.

The Emperor Justinian was one of the ablest of the Byzantine emperors, equally brilliant as a scholar, a soldier, an administrator and a theologian; it was he who consolidated and directed the empire after the final collapse of Rome. But Justinian did not get everything right; in 532 a riot in the city – originally between the two rival sporting factions, the 'Blues' and the 'Greens' – became a full-scale rebellion against government oppression and extortion. The 'Nika' Rebellion was eventually crushed by Justinian's legendary general, Belisarius, with the massacre of some 30,000 rioters in the Hippodrome, but much of Constantine's majestic city lay in ruins.

Justinian enthusiastically set about rebuilding the city as he wanted it. There had been a church of Aghia Sofia on the same spot since 350, but it had collapsed in earthquakes, burned down, and now lay destroyed by the mob. The new church was to be the crowning glory of Justinian's reign, a church 'such as has not been seen since Adam, nor will ever be seen again'. Accordingly, Justinian sent for two learned men from Anatolia; Anthemius of Tralles and Isidorus of Miletus; they were actually physicists and mathematicians rather than architects. However, by 532 the plans were ready and a team of 10,000 skilled workmen was assembled. The church was completed in five years under the personal supervision of the emperor. No scaffolding was used, instead the work was carried out from mounds of earth piled beside the walls. It is said that the emperor, in order to finish the church in record time, divided the workforce in two, promising a bonus for the faster. When it was finished, Justinian entered his church, saying 'Glory be to

God, who has judged me worthy to accomplish such a work, and to surpass even thee, O Solomon.'

The church was consecrated in 537, becoming the principal place of worship in the first city of Christianity, along with Rome, for over six centuries. In 1204, when the Fourth Crusaders turned on their Christian brethren and sacked Constantinople, the church was utterly desecrated; a whore was placed on the Patriarch's gilded throne, singing bawdy songs and drinking wine from the holy chalices. In 1261, the Greeks took their capital back and reconsecrated the church.

Nearly 200 years later, in 1453, when Mehmet the Conqueror's Ottoman Turks entered the city, after two months of siege and bloody fighting, the soldiers were given *carte blanche* to loot to their hearts content, but had strict instructions to leave all buildings intact. The conqueror himself waited a day before his triumphal entry into the city, and then he proceeded straight to Aghia Sofia. Dismounting at the door, he entered in silent awe. The magnificent church was empty, the thousands of citizens who had sought refuge there having already been led away to their various fates. Immediately, Mehmet ordered that the church should be reconsecrated as a mosque; an Imam pronounced the appropriate formulae, and the great Christian church became the greatest mosque of the Ottoman Caliphate. For 470 years it remained a mosque until, in 1935, Atatürk boldly declared that it should become a museum.

The building you see today does not look exactly as it would have done in 537. Part of the main dome collapsed in an earthquake 20 years after it was built; during rebuilding the dome was raised 6 m and the diameter reduced, in order to redirect the powerful outward thrust. A number of subsequent earthquakes destroyed parts of the church, but the main structure has survived. The four minarets were added at various times during the Ottoman years, as were many of the buttresses that distort the outside shape today. The outside is undeniably magnificent, but it's not to everybody's taste; many find it heavy and ungainly, the proportions displeasing.

Entering through the Imperial Gate, from the cross-vaulted narthex, you find yourself at the west end of the nave. Above you the great dome, supported by two huge semi-domes, hovers over an immensity of space. The top of the central dome, said by the Byzantines to be 'suspended from Heaven by a golden chain', is 56 m from the ground – about the height of a 15-storey building. It is supported by four great columns in a square 31 m to a side; the vast space created by this arrangement, makes Aghia Sofia one of the most awesome buildings on earth. The great thing is that you don't have to know about architecture, or even to be interested in it, to be thunderstruck by the vastness of the space; it impresses you in the way that a great mountain, an abyss or a cataract impresses you – yet this wonder of the world was built by man over 1,000 years ago.

Justinian spared no expense in the building and decoration of his church; the materials he used were a reflection of the great wealth and extent of the Byzantine Empire in the sixth century. Columns of porphyry were shipped from Egypt, green stone pillars from the Gymnasium at Ephesus, marble pillars from Baalbek, while pagan temples all around the Mediterranean were stripped of their columns and capitals. Only the finest materials went into the construction. Exquisite many-coloured marble slabs adorn the walls, skilfully cut to give a mirror-image of the grain. On the walls of the galleries are some fine mosaics, although the activities of the Iconoclasts have deprived us of most of these.

Today, it is all rather bare and austere beneath the great dome. There's no furniture or carpets, just a floor of polished stone. This may heighten the impression of space, but you must use your imagination to picture the sumptuous wealth of gold, silver, precious jewels and fine hangings with which the church was decked before the Crusaders arrived. 'I stake my word that never had any army gained so much plunder in the whole history of the world' wrote a contemporary French traveller.

To return to the real world, a shady TEA-GARDEN would fit the bill; there is just such a one by the south-west wall of Aghia Sofia, looking across the garden towards the Blue Mosque.

BLUE MOSQUE

The mosque of Sultan Ahmet was built by Mehmet Ağa in 1617, at the end of the 'Classical' period of Ottoman architecture. It stands across the garden from Aghia Sofia, on the spot where the former palace of the Byzantine emperors stood – unfortunately nothing of the palace remains. The Blue Mosque, as it is known, is one of the most majestic of the 'Sultan's Mosques' and contains one of the city's largest religious complexes.

The mosque is set in a great marble-paved courtyard, in the middle of which is a *şadırvan*; a domed gallery runs around the sides. Take your time looking at the outside, for one of the qualities of this mosque is the beauty and harmony of the 'domescapes'. Framed in the arched entrance, you see tier upon tier of domes, rising finally to the huge central dome, an impression of colossal mass, delicately balanced and soaring

Istanbul mosque

upwards. The central mass is complemented by six graceful minarets – it's the only mosque with six minarets.

Inside you discover why it's called the 'Blue Mosque'; for the massive piers and columns, walls and domes are gloriously decked with tiles of green and blue – 21,000 of the finest examples of Iznik faience (ceramics), painted and fired by skilled craftsmen brought from distant Persia. The designs are mostly floral motifs – carnations, peonies, tulips and vines, as well as complex arabesques and geometric patterns, swirling upwards from the richly-carpeted floor to the bluish haze above. Here, the light is suffused with the vivid blue of the tiles, which seems to emphasise the vastness and peace of the interior. Note the four massive but graceful fluted columns; these are needed to support the mass of domes high above. The interior of the Blue Mosque is undoubtedly the most striking of Istanbul's mosques.

Sokollu Mehmet Paşa Camii

If you want to see more examples of fine tile decoration in a less awesome setting, try the Mehmet Paşa Camii, 400 m west of the Blue Mosque in the back streets of Sultanahmet. The mosque itself is simple and harmonious. It was built by Sinan, Süleyman the Magnificent's great architect, for the wife of the Vizier Mehmet Paşa, in 1571. The tiles here are, again, from Iznik, and were the very best available. The tomato-red, fired into the glaze in livid dollops, is one of the major achievements of the Iznik workshops. Look at the patterns. There are whole murals composed of tiles, coloured arabesques and intricate calligraphy, although flower patterns are the dominant theme. You'll see plenty of wonderful tile-work in other mosques all over Turkey, but nothing quite like this. Note the tiled spire on the *minber* – it's unique.

Also worth a visit for enthusiasts of fine tiles, is the RÜSTEM PAŞA CAMII – the next mosque west of Yeni Camii, on the waterfront.

Küçük Aghia Sofia

From Mehmet Paşa, walk 200 m down Mehmet Paşa Sokak towards the sea. Here is Küçük Aghia Sofia (Little Aghia Sofia), or the CHURCH OF ST SERGIUS AND ST BACCHUS. Apart from being one of the finest examples of Byzantine architecture remaining in Istanbul, it is a beautiful church. Built by Justinian in 527, it consists of an octagon contained in a square, surmounted by a flattened dome, an early form of Byzantine church architecture, of which very little survives. Within the great arch on each side of the octagon, are three smaller arches, supported by two marble pillars. Note the typical ornate Byzantine capitals, decorated with acanthus leaves. The Iconoclasts have left their mark here too, destroying all the murals with which the church would have been adorned – not altogether a bad thing here, for it simplifies the building. Saints Sergius and Bacchus, incidentally, were Roman soldiers martyred for their adoption of Christianity.

Ibrahim Paşa Sarayi

Back to the Blue Mosque and across the HIPPODROME, where the chariot-races of Constantinople were held, is the Ibrahim Paşa Sarayı. This imposing palace was once the town-house of Süleyman's brilliant and beloved friend, the Grand Vizier, Ibrahim Paşa. Jealous of the close friendship between the two men, and of Ibrahim's success, the sultan's Russian wife, Roxelana, turned her husband's heart against Ibrahim, and at the peak of his career – from slave-boy to Grand Vizier – he was murdered. Today his home houses the MUSEUM OF TURKISH AND ISLAMIC ART. It is a fine museum, well laid out, containing many works of great beauty – pottery, stone and wood carving, Koran-boxes, Korans, carpets, and a section on Turkish Folk Culture – and in a beautiful setting, with its fine terrace overlooking the *At Meydan* (Hippodrome) and the Blue

Mosque; but it seems a pity that there is nothing left of the original furnishings and decoration of the palace, the most magnificent built during Ottoman times for anyone other than a sultan.

ALMAN ÇEŞME

The three columns before the Ibrahim Paşa Sarayı, the EGYPTIAN OBELISK, the SERPENT COLUMN, and the COLUMN OF CONSTANTINE VII, mark the central reservation of the Hippodrome. Further north is the *Alman Çeşme* (German Fountain) – presented to Sultan Abdul Hamid by Kaiser Wilhelm II in 1895. It's not a bad fountain, but its chief claim to fame is as a commemoration of the visit of the Kaiser and his Empress. The Empress was formally introduced to the *Kızlar Ağa*, the Chief Eunuch and one of the most powerful dignitaries of the Empire. Stumped for conversation, she asked him . . . 'and was your father a eunuch too?'

FIRUZ AĞA CAMII

If you turn left onto the main street, DIVAN YOLU, you will see on your left the mosque of Firuz Ağa. This is a very simple mosque – a dome on a square block, with a simple portico – the basis of all future Ottoman mosques. It is interesting to compare its simplicity with the more complex developments that followed it, for it was one of the first mosques built in the city, in 1491.

THE CISTERNS

Nearby are two of the great underground cisterns, BINBIRD-IREK and YEREBATANSARAY both of which can be visited, but which have been undergoing repairs recently. These enormous underground reservoirs are over 1,500 years old and were built to serve the water system of Constantine's city; over 80 have been unearthed. Yerebatansaray is still full of water; you used to be able to glide among the vistas of marble columns in a rowing boat – a cool and silent haven from the city above. Binbirdirek is full of rubble and earth; for many years it was used as a silk factory, its cool humid atmosphere ideal for the process. The cisterns are magnificent, and big, though not perhaps as big as some observers would have us believe – in 1830, it is said, two Englishmen set out across the cistern in a boat, and were never seen again. Later, another Englishman swore that he had rowed in a straight line for two hours, without reaching the end – a reflection rather of his skill as an oarsman, than of the dimensions of the cistern, which measure 150 m by 75 m.

Topkapı Sarayı

When Mehmet the Conqueror entered Constantinople in 1453, he found a city in ruins. An enfeebled and venal administration was attempting to order the affairs of a population decimated by plague, war and the constant strife between rival Imperial factions. A mere 50,000 people were living among the weeds and ruins of a city built for a million. The great palace of the Byzantine emperors was little more than a pile of rubble. As Mehmet walked among the ruins of the once-glorious city, he is said to have quoted from the Persian poet, Saadi;

The spider spins his web in the Palace of the Caesars,
And the owl calls the watches on the Towers of Afrasiab

The first thing to do when revitalising a conquered city, is to build a new palace; the huge influx of workers, artists, masons, merchants, victuallers, etc., that this entails, gives the economy a tremendous boost, and the fruits of successful wars, conducted on distant frontiers, pay the bills. The first palace of the Ottoman sultans was built where the Süleymaniye mosque stands today, but 15 years later, in 1468, Mehmet ordered the construction of a new palace to stand on the Acropolis (defensive hill), overlooking his new city. From now, until the official Imperial Residence moved to DOLMABAHÇE in 1856, the TOPKAPI SARAYI was the centre of the Ottoman world. Mehmet himself continued to live with his wives, his eunuchs and his harem, in the old palace. This custom continued until the time of Süleyman the Magnificent, when the sultan's domestic arrangements were moved to Topkapı, at the instigation of his wife Roxelana, who saw an advantage in being nearer the *Divan* (government). From this time, with the harem and the eunuchs becoming more and more involved in the affairs of government, dates the beginning of the decline of the Ottoman Empire.

The wealth lavished upon the palace almost defies belief; it was provided by extortionate taxes and tributes, crippling the economy of the whole empire. The stories of life within the walls of this 'Gilded Cage' present a fascinating pageant of cruelty, horror and degradation, against a background of brilliance and the exquisite refinements of a high civilisation. Today the privilege of entering the palace, for centuries denied to all but a chosen few, is open to anybody. In high season it gets very crowded, so much so that it is often difficult to see the exhibits for the press of the crowd. (It is best to go out of season, but, failing that, try 9.00 a.m. on a weekday morning.) However disagreeable and irritating the crowds may be, you should not miss the opportunity to view the beautifully restored remains of this almost legendary splendour.

The BAB-I-HÜMAYUN, to the south-east of Aghia Sofia, is the first gate of the palace of Topkapı, leading into the COURT OF THE JANISSARIES; anyone could enter here, but silence had to be observed, on pain of the 'Bastinadoe' (a cruel beating on the soles of the feet), lest the slumber of princes be disturbed. On the left is the church of AGHIA EIRENE, now used as a museum and concert hall.

Buy a ticket from the kiosk on the right and proceed to the BAB-I-SELAM – the Gate of Salutations; passing through this gate you will be in the Seraglio proper.

Do not enter this gate lightly. It is the gate to the court of an empire that for 500 years ruled half the world. Look to your right, and see the EXECUTIONER'S FOUNTAIN, where the executioner would wash his hands and sword after decapitating a commoner – a silken bowstring was used to garotte those of noble birth, so as not to shed the 'Blood Royal'. This job, curiously enough, fell to the head gardener, along with the organising of ceremonies and processions and the provisioning of the palace and the army. Through this gate you must walk, for none but the sultan was permitted to ride. Now there are turnstiles and on the other side is the COURTYARD OF THE DIVAN. Here, shaded by majestic cypresses and plane-trees, the affairs of the Imperial court were conducted with elaborate pomp and ceremony while the tame birds and gazelles that roamed free in the courtyard doubtless looked on with gentle curiosity.

Along the south side of the court are the enormous KITCHENS which served the palace – in which, according to some sources, some 200 cooks laboured. This does not seem unreasonable when you consider that the palace housed about 5,000 under normal circumstances, and up to 15,000 on special occasions. In one year, observed an early traveller, the court consumed 30,000 oxen, 20,000 calves, 60,000 sheep, 16,000 lambs, 10,000 kids and 100,000 turkeys. This implies, from a rough calculation, that every inhabitant of the palace would have to eat six oxen, four calves, twelve sheep, three lambs and twenty turkeys every year! Today the kitchens house one of the world's major collections of CHINESE AND JAPANESE PORCELAIN, although the two end chambers are reserved for a display of the gargantuan kitchenware that was used to prepare the food of the Janissaries.

Across the courtyard are the IMPERIAL STABLES, housing an opulent collection of carriages and harness.

On the north side of the court is the HAREM; you must pay extra to visit this part of the palace, and you are obliged to join a group and be herded around in a most undignified and unrewarding manner. However, this is the only way you can get to see the harem, and it is worth seeing – some of the finest buildings in the palace are here. When Süleyman and Roxelana moved here, the harem was simple and built mainly of wood; but it burned down on a number of occasions, and, as it was rebuilt and added to by successive incumbents, it became the disorganised collection of buildings we see today.

The harem (an Arabic word, meaning 'forbidden') is said to contain some 400 rooms, many of extraordinary beauty, spread among a convoluted maze of kiosks, corridors and courtyards. There are baths, gardens, dining rooms, a swimming pool, living quarters, a laundry and guardrooms and mosques for the eunuchs. Despite the beauty and opulence of the surroundings, one cannot help feeling a real sense of loneliness and desolation in this gilded cage, where the Imperial wives and concubines lived their narrowly circumscribed lives, closely guarded by 'those pernicious vermin of the East', the eunuchs. For centuries this was probably the most inaccessible building in the world. The last of the women left here in 1909.

The guided tour takes you through only a very few of the rooms of the harem, which is built on several floors and, at its peak, was home to 1,200 women. You do not, for instance, see the *Kafes* – the Cage – where the younger brothers of reigning sultans would spend their entire lives, confined to a few rooms of the harem, knowing and seeing only the concubines and eunuchs. Before the initiation of this custom, the sultan's younger brothers were strangled with a silken bowstring. Barbaric though it seems, the practice did achieve the desired effect of avoiding endless wars of succession, which would probably have resulted in the deaths of far more people in far more gruesome ways. It is debatable, though, which practice was the more cruel, for those who were fortunate enough to emerge from the *Kafes* at all were often illiterate, neurotic imbeciles – twisted by a life of pampered luxury, carnal excess and constant fear of the gardener with his silken bowstring. Those who did leave the cage would become sultan – no wonder the empire declined! The guides who take you round the harem tend to emphasise the more positive aspects of the institution, and quite right too – but one should bear in mind that the refinement of these beautiful surroundings has often cloaked deeds of unspeakable cruelty, brutality and debauchery.

DIVAN

The building beneath the square tower is the HALL OF THE DIVAN – KUBBEALTI, where the government sat. Above the seat of the Grand Vizier is a grille through which the sultan could observe the proceedings unbeknown to his ministers. Later, in the throne room, an account of the business would be solemnly reported to the sultan, by a high minister, who would have been unsure whether or not the sultan was already in the know. You can imagine the chastening and stultifying effect that this must have had upon the affairs of government.

ARZ ODASI

At the head of the Court of the Divan is the BAB-I-SAADET, the Gate of Felicity, an imposing entrance designed to intimidate further those supplicants who were not already utterly overcome by fear and awe. Behind the gate is the AUDIENCE HALL – *Arz Odası* – where the sultan himself sat in ostentatious pomp and on rare occasions, received ambassadors. One of the very few ordinary mortals who entered this chamber was Lord Byron. He was presented to Sultan Mahmut II by the British Ambassador, Stratford Canning. All supplicants, no matter how exalted, were subjected to thoroughly degrading treatment. The ambassador, no matter who he was, would be grabbed unceremoniously at the gate by a couple of immense eunuchs, and bundled into the sultan's presence; if he were tardy or unenthusiastic in his grovelling obeisances, a pudgy hand on his neck would thrust his head to the floor several times before he was permitted to state his business. No matter how perfect the ambassador's command of the language, the sultan was only to be addressed through an intepreter; his Imperial ears were not to be soiled by the speech of ordinary mortals and especially not that of infidels. When the sultan tired of the audience, the victim would be grovelled once more, and then dragged out backwards by the eunuchs; you didn't turn your back on a sultan.

To the right of the Gate of Felicity is the pavilion containing the greatest treasures of the palace: the bow, the sword, the Holy Mantle and some hairs from the beard of the Prophet Mohammed himself. This is understandably a very holy place.

Treasury

On the south side of the Divan Courtyard is the TREASURY. It contains the most stunning display of wealth and vanity, but also of skilled craftsmanship and artistry, that you are ever likely to see. The halls are overflowing with jewel-encrusted thrones, priceless tea- and coffee-sets, bangles and jewellery of inestimable value, glittering diamonds and gleaming gold and silver. The main attractions are the SPOONMAKER'S DIAMOND, an 86 carat monster, the size of a big fist, and an uncut emerald weighing 3 kg. The wealth displayed here is easier to grasp when you remember that one fifth of *all* the spoils of war was the sultan's due. This made war worth waging – as long as you played by simple rules, as the Ottomans did, and consistently won.

Next to the treasury is a room lined with display-cases; each case is devoted to a particular sultan and contains a portrait, a robe, a suit of clothes, letters and personal effects – right through from Mehmet II to Abdul Hamid II. This is a fascinating collection.

Continuing through the Audience Hall, you reach the Third Court, where only the sultan and his most intimate minions were allowed. Here are beautiful marble terraces with elaborate KIOSKS, set among pools of water with fountains; particularly fine are the BAGHDAD and the REVAN KIOSKS, with their lovely views of the Bosphorus. You'll find the restaurant here. It's quite good but gets very busy at mealtimes, with tables often booked solid by organised tours. Get there early if possible.

Beyazit Camii

As DIVAN YOLU heads west out of Sultanahmet district, it opens into the broad BEYAZIT SQUARE, with its flocks of pigeons, waiting for you to buy a tray of seed from the bird-seed sellers. The pigeon, in common with the cat, is a favoured creature of Islam. The Prophet was particularly fond of both. This is one of the liveliest places in Istanbul. Water-sellers and shoe-shine boys ply their trade all over the square. All manner of snacks are on sale from little kiosks or from portable trays, and tea-sellers, bent double under the weight of huge tea urns, dispense tiny cups of Turkish tea. On one side of the square are the monumental gates of the UNIVERSITY; on the other is the BEYAZIT II CAMII, otherwise known as the Mosque of the Dove. This is the oldest surviving sultan's mosque in the city. It was built for Beyazıt II, the Conqueror's son, in 1506. The design is rather like a simplified Aghia Sofia, and is one of the finest examples of Classical Ottoman architecture. It is noted for the beauty of its courtyard, with the lovely *şadırvan* in the centre, and the galleries with their 24 small domes. Next to the mosque is the SAHAFLAR ÇARŞISI, the OLD BOOK MARKET, a shady, open-air market where you can spend hours browsing. Many of the books on sale today are guidebooks to Istanbul, but there is also a wealth of other interesting books, from Korans, ancient and modern, to esoteric treatises on the mysteries of hydraulics, in German.

Nearby is a fine TEA-GARDEN, shaded by huge spreading planes, and popular with the students from the university across the square. The TOWER rising from the university grounds is the tower of the former War Ministry.

KAPALI ÇARŞI

Even today, 500 years after it was first built, the Grand Bazaar of Istanbul is the world's greatest concentration of shops and stalls under one roof, and still one of the most richly varied markets in the world. Mehmet the Conqueror built it in 1461, as part of his plan to revitalise the moribund city he had just conquered. The original market was attached to the mosque of Aghia Sofia and the revenues provided for the upkeep of that venerable building, and the maintenance of the charitable institutions with which it was surrounded during Ottoman times.

As a stimulus to trade in the city, the new market was a huge success, for within 100 years of its foundation, it was the largest market in the world. There were over 4,000 shops, along with warehouses, workshops, trade-schools, inns, *lokantas*, mosques, fountains, a police station, and a fire service.

Architecturally, the most interesting parts of the market are the original CEVAHIR BEDESTENI and the SANDAL BEDES-TENI, still much the same as when they were built in 1461. All-covered markets were built around a BEDESTEN; in earlier Ottoman times the stalls of traders in precious goods – gold, silver, silks, etc. – would have been here. In the absence of banks, the wealthy of the city came to deposit their valuables with the merchants of the *bedesten*, which was equipped with strong-boxes and patrolled by market guards at night. Eventually the *bedesten* became the repository of enormous wealth, with its own accredited guards and porters. Attracted by this wealth, other merchants would establish themselves in the surrounding area, and thus the market grew. As early as the time of Mehmet the Conqueror, there was an organisation for the protection of consumers; market police, the forerunners of today's blue-uniformed police, would patrol the market streets, checking weights and measures. Anyone found giving short measure would be publicly beaten in front of his stall – very bad for business.

Each of the market's 67 streets is known by the name of the guild that used to operate there – Fur Cap Makers', Slipper-makers', Pearl Merchants', Cobblers', Mirror-makers', etc. And even today each street tends to specialise in one particular commodity, as is generally the custom in the East.

The market is an irresistible magnet for tourist and Turk alike, and, although it's not the cheapest place to buy, there are still bargains to be found; whether you plan to buy or not, you shouldn't miss it.

But the delights of the KAPALI ÇARSI do not end under its roof, for as the market grew, many merchants, too late to claim a place inside, set up their businesses in the surrounding *Hans*. a *Han* was a simple inn or a whole Caravanserai – a resting place for travellers and their caravans, with stabling and fodder for the horses and camels, rooms for the merchants, mosques, workshops and coffee-houses. There are still dozens of *Hans* in the streets surrounding the Kapalı Çarşı; often they are buildings of distinctive charm and beauty, with cobbled, tree-shaded yards – see particularly the ZINCIRLI HAN, for goldsmiths and jewellers (entrance from inside the market). One particularly good *Han* to visit, especially for those who enjoy a smoke, is the ATIK ALI PAŞA HANI. You will find it off the main YENIÇERILER CADDESI, near ÇEMBERLITAŞ, the Banded Stone Column. Here amongst the carpet dealers are several little tea-gardens, where the customers are provided with *narghiles*, elaborate Turkish water pipes.

SÜLEYMANIYE CAMII

On the hill overlooking the Golden Horn, 500 m north of the Beyazıt mosque, is the stupendous Süleymaniye mosque. If you see no other mosque in Istanbul, you should see this one. It's not the biggest, but it's certainly the finest example of Ottoman architecture in the city. It was built between 1550 and 1557 by Süleyman the Magnificent and his great architect Sinan. Süleyman had been on the throne for 30 years when he built this mosque, so he was determined that it should be a monument worthy of his own magnificence – of which he had no small opinion. But, to be fair, it should be pointed out that the building of a mosque was not merely an act of self-glorification. A mosque was also for the people; anyone, from the highest to the lowest could enter and pray; indeed the Süleymaniye and its courtyard are said to have been able to accommodate 27,000 of the faithful at any one time – 5,000 in the prayer-hall alone. There were no 'High' or 'Low-church' mosques; even the sultan would worship in the same mosque as the common people, although his worship would be conducted in a screened 'Royal Box'. Most mosques have a screened 'Women's Gallery' at the back, where women can pray without distracting the faithful, though the separate gallery in the Süleymaniye is for the nobility.

One of the five sacred obligations of Islam is the giving of alms to the poor; this was the secondary function of a mosque. Built around the mosque and its courtyard, with its *Shadırvan* for washing and drinking, would be a *Külliye*, a complex that would consist of a religious school, a primary school, a public bath, a hospital, a kitchen for the poor, a hostel, and finally the *Türbe*, or Tomb, of the founder of the mosque and his family. All these facilities were free, a considerable improvement on contemporary Western Europe, where the poor had to look out for themselves.

But how was this admirable charity to be paid for? The cost of the building of the mosque and its *Külliye* would be born by the founder. The founder and other wealthy patrons would also give the mosque some means of support – an endowment called a *waqf*. A *waqf* bequest usually took the form of houses, shops, whole streets, land or vineyards, the rent or produce of which supported the *Külliye*. The Süleymaniye itself was endowed by HÜRREM SULTAN (Roxelana), the sultan's wife, with 'a lake and all the lands around Tiberias, including the fisheries, the hot medicinal springs and their famous baths' – a fair income.

It was not only mosques and *Külliyes* that were financed by *waqf* bequests, but also 'libraries and schools, hospitals and *hamams*, hospices, soup-kitchens and laundries, bridges and fountains, orphanages, repayment of debts for imprisoned debtors, burial for the indigent, clothes for the aged, rice for the birds, springtime picnics for schoolchildren, as well as aid to soldiers and their families, and the construction and mainte-nance of forts and ships for the defence of the realm of Islam.'

You enter the complex through the huge courtyard, surrounded by domed galleries, with their marble pillars taken from Byzantine palaces and other Classical sites – the Ottomans never got the hang of making their own pillars. At each of the four corners of the complex is a tall minaret, two with two balconies, and two with three; the four minarets signifying that Süleyman was the fourth sultan to reign in

Istanbul, the ten balconies, that he was the tenth of the Ottoman line.

The interior is simple and uncluttered, but vastly spacious. The proportions of the walls, pillars and high domes are in perfect harmony. What decorations there are, are restrained, simple and exquisitely executed. There is not the flamboyance of decoration found in the Blue Mosque. Note the stained glass by a craftsman, known as Ibrahim the Drunkard, and the lovely calligraphy by Ahmet Karahisarı, the best there was.

As in most mosques, there is a great iron hoop suspended on chains from the central dome; this gives the impression of a false ceiling, heightening the sense of heavenly space above. The hoop, nowadays set with electric lights, would formerly have been lit with oil-lamps, festooned with the first sheaves of corn from the harvest and hung with ostrich eggs – pious gifts from those who had made the pilgrimage to Mecca and an effective measure against spiders. The carpets, some of them 20 m long, were donated by members of the congregation.

Sinan really excelled himself here, and though he considered his greatest achievement to be the Selimiye at Edirne, it was overlooking the Süleymaniye that he chose to live and die. He built his house just to the north-east of the mosque, and his tomb is still there, in the corner of the garden. It is a pretty tomb with a tiny dome and a public drinking-fountain.

To the east of the mosque are the TOMBS OF SÜLEYMAN and ROXELANA, the former with its dome set with glittering constellations of jewels. The former *medrese* on the south side is now a MUSEUM OF OTTOMAN ART.

KARIYE CAMII

Out by the city walls, near the EDIRNEKAPI, is the pretty little church of St Saviour in Chora (meaning countryside). As with St Martin-in-the-Fields in London's Trafalgar Square, this church was originally surrounded by green fields. The church was built in 1080, on the instructions of Maria Doukaina, mother-in-law of the Emperor Alexis I Comnenus. Severely damaged by earthquakes and ravaged by the Crusaders, it was lovingly restored and redecorated by Theodore Metochites, the 'Grand Logothete', at the beginning of the fourteenth century.

Metochites was one of the greatest men of his day and a leading light in the Byzantine Renaissance. He was prime minister, lord of the treasury, an eminent theologian, a philosopher, astronomer, and a poet. In his spare time he restored the church, adding much of the building that still stands. The wonderful paintings and mosaics date from his time too. But in Byzantium, as everywhere else, the heights of power were precarious, and when Andronicus III Palaeologus usurped the throne, the Grand Logothete was reduced to penury and exiled. He was later allowed to return to the city, provided that he enter the monastery of the church he loved as a humble monk; this he did, and lived there until he died in 1332.

For a long time St Saviour's was the repository of a famous icon attributed to St Luke; this icon was paraded solemnly round the walls of the city during times of trouble. It proved effective against Murat II when he laid siege to Constantinople in 1428, but it didn't work in 1453, and when the church was pillaged by Mehmet the Conqueror's army, the holy icon was lost and it has never been seen since. After the conquest, the church was converted to a mosque, with the addition of a small minaret, and the unaccountable bricking up of some of the arches, but fortunately there was no wholesale destruction of the paintings and mosaics.

Today, thanks to the painstaking care and devotion lavished upon the church by the Byzantine Society of America, the mosaics and paintings are preserved. They are without doubt the finest surviving examples of late Byzantine art anywhere. There is such a profusion of beautiful works on the walls, vaults and domes, that it would be impossible to describe them all here; but probably the finest piece, and the most famous – described as 'one of the most beautiful paintings in the world' – is 'THE HARROWING OF HELL'. You'll find it inside the semi-dome at the end of the parecclesion – the Side-church. This shows Christ leading Adam and Eve by the hand from the pit beneath the broken gates of Hell. Satan, in the form of an Ethiopian, lies bound at his feet, in a dark world of shattered locks and keys; a host of saints looks on. Even if you find early Byzantine art a bit fusty and dry, this is a different thing altogether – graceful, and full of life, movement and passion. The Kariye Camii, as it's known, should not be missed.

MUSEUMS

From the Court of the Janissaries in the Topkapı Sarayı, a road leads down the hill to the MUSEUM OF THE ANCIENT ORIENT and the MUSEUM OF ARCHAEOLOGY. The road is a museum in itself for all the columns, capitals, steles, sarcophagi and statues that couldn't be squeezed into the museum buildings are lying here in splendid disarray.

The Museum of Archaeology should not be missed. It contains the best of everything from all the Classical sites of Asia Minor – a huge collection, from obscure ancient gods through to the noble periods of Greek and Roman art. The collection of SARCOPHAGI is one of the finest in the world. It includes one that was said to contain the remains of Alexander the Great. (It doesn't apparently, but it is a stupendous sarcophagus for all that.) The carvings on the sides depict scenes from the life of Alexander.

The MUSEUM OF THE ANCIENT ORIENT goes back a little further, with a wealth of HITTITE ART, including the fine stone lions guarding the entrance and a large and fascinating collection of works from Assyria, Mesopotamia and Babylon.

The third museum in this complex is the ÇINILI KÖŞK, now the MUSEUM OF TURKISH TILES AND CERAMICS. The building itself, once part of the Topkapı Palace, was built as a pleasure-pavilion, during the time of Mehmet the Conqueror. It is one of the most beautiful of all the secular buildings of Ottoman Istanbul. Most of the tiles that once covered the exterior have disappeared now, but the fine, tall pillars with their ogival arches remain. Beautifully proportioned and somewhat exotic they are unique in Turkey and reminiscent of earlier Persian architecture. The tiles inside, both on the walls and on display, are a fine introduction to this form of decoration.

FOUNTAINS

There are many more monuments in Istanbul than you could hope to visit in a month at the run; there is the mighty AQUEDUCT OF VALENS, plenty more CISTERNS, a hundred Ottoman HAMAMS, many still in use, and a thousand FOUNTAINS. On the corner of every street and alley, in every courtyard, square and park there are fountains. There are proud Imperial fountains, like the elaborate Rococo SEBIL OF AHMET III, by the main entrance to the Topkapı Sarayı; then there are the humble spigots set into a marble niche in a wall, and a whole host in between. There are books devoted entirely to the fountains of Istanbul. For the Turk, from the highest to the lowest, the sweetest repose is to sit quietly by trickling water. But the great thing about fountains in Turkey is that they fulfil a practical need; they are not there just to be admired from afar, they are for drinking, cooling off and washing the dust from one's feet, neck and hands.

BEYOĞLU

But there is more to Istanbul than monuments. As an antidote to a day spent absorbing the lofty notions of artists and architects, there is nothing better than to plunge into the morass of everyday life. This, Istanbul offers in plenty. It seethes around you all day long in the streets and alleys and squares. For a concentrated dose of one of the many aspects of Istanbul life, cross the GALATA BRIDGE and climb the hill – or take the TÜNEL (subway) if it's hot – to ISTIKLAL CADDESI.

Istiklal Caddesi is the hub of the old European quarter of the city, Beyoğlu. It runs from the top of the Galata hill to TAKSIM, the bright new commercial district, where the airlines have their offices, and the opulent bulks of the international hotels brighten the skyline. All along the street, among the great variety of shops enticing you with their myriad wares, are hundreds of restaurants, *lokantas, pastahanes,* beer-halls and tea-shops to fit every taste and pocket. There are also churches, Greek, Russian and Armenian, as well as the imposing edifices of the foreign legations and embassies; for this was once the domain of the bankers, merchants and ambassadors of the Western nations.

Parallel to Istiklal, and to the west, runs MEŞRÜTIYET CADDESI; here are two of the best hotels in the city, the BÜYÜK LONDRA, and the famous PERA PALAS. The Pera was built to accommodate the well-heeled Edwardian travellers who had made the journey to Istanbul on the old Orient Express, for in those days there was not the variety of opulent hotels there are today. The Edwardian grandeur has faded a little, but the atmosphere is still superb, and a night in one of the huge, plush rooms, or even a drink at the bar, is an experience you will remember.

On the Bosphorus side, a steep hill falls away to the waterfront, crowded with decaying tenements; above the cobbled street hang tangled webs of telephone-lines and strings of laundry gathering smuts in the poor air. Even here though, in one of the sadder parts of the city, there are little corners of curious and whimsical beauty – a photographer's paradise.

NIGHTCLUBS

Leading off Istiklal itself are dozens of streets crowded with nightclubs; almost unnoticeable during the day, they bloom as dusk falls and the neon signs are switched on. There are hundreds to choose from: belly-dancing shows, cabarets, strippers, folk-dancing, discos and just plain bars. If you want to see a belly-dancer perform her astonishing feats of abdominal dexterity, there are many places to choose from. The shows vary from dazzling to quite laughable. In order to get an idea of what it is all about, try the CARAVANSERAI in CUMHURIYET CADDESI. Although this is the big club where the tourists are all taken, the food, the music and the show are all of a very high standard. Take this as your yardstick and then explore the Istiklal clubs – try the Elize, Olimpia or Balim among others. In general, Istanbul is a good place to go nightclubbing, for although the clubs are not as plush and sophisticated as those of Western cities, they are much cheaper and quite often a good deal more pleasant.

Çiçek Pasajı

On the west corner of the bend in Istiklal Caddesi is an L-shaped alley called ÇIÇEK PASAJI – Flower Alley. Here you can wind up and get in the mood for visiting the nightclubs nearby. The alley is lined with beer-halls, their chairs and tables spilling onto the pavements. Sellers of the choicest morsels weave among the exuberant crowds of students and merry-makers; *mezes* of incomparable seafood are yours for a reasonable price. Gipsy dancers somehow clear a space and whirl to the accompaniment of wandering street-musicians; poets declaim; the beer and wine flows freely. Go early, say 6.00 or 7.00 p.m., and watch it build up steam, for after 9.00 p.m., when the tourist buses arrive, the prices double and the atmosphere gets watered down a bit. Don't miss Çiçek Pasajı; there are other lively places in Istanbul, but this is the best.

Galata Tower

Between the southern end of Istiklal and the Galata Bridge, you can't help but notice the GALATA TOWER. In the daytime you can go up in a lift for a stupendous, if somewhat alarming, view of Istanbul. The tower was built by the Genoese in 1348 as part of the fortifications of their concession in the Byzantine city. It is said that the great chain that closed the Golden Horn was raised and lowered by a giant capstan here. At night it becomes a restaurant and a nightclub with a wonderful view over the lights of the city. South of the tower, on the slope leading down to the bridge, is Istanbul's major RED LIGHT DISTRICT.

Restaurants

There are so many thousands of restaurants of every type in Istanbul, that it would be futile to try and give a comprehensive list, but the following guidelines may be useful. Istiklal is well supplied with eating establishments – special and famous are the HACI BABA, with its terrace overlooking the garden of the GREEK ORTHODOX CHURCH, and the DÖRT MEVSIM, Four Seasons, near the Swedish Consulate. For 'international' restaurants, stick to the area round TAKSIM and the big hotels; here you can find French, Chinese and high quality but expensive Turkish restaurants – also fast food joints. Down on the waterfront at KARAKÖY, Beyoğlu side of the Galata Bridge, there are several FISH RESTAURANTS, the best of which is the LIMAN LOKANTASI in the big waterfront Maritime Office block; the others here tend to be rather over-priced and ordinary. There are however some excellent *pastahanes* in this area.

For a concentration of FISH RESTAURANTS, the best place to go is KUMKAPI, on the Marmara slope of Sultanahmet. Here, in what used to be a fishing harbour and village, there are dozens of restaurants; the food is excellent, the prices moderate and the atmosphere incomparable, with tables on the street, a great deal of exuberance and strolling musicians – this is the best place in Istanbul to eat, or just while away an evening with beer, wine or Rakı.

Equally good are the restaurants in the BOSPHORUS VILLAGES; here you eat delicious seafood in little restaurants right on the waterfront. ANADOLU KAVAĞI has particularly good restaurants, but it's a long way to go – two hours on a steamer. Try ARNAVUTKÖY, RUMELI HISAR, KANLICA, YENI-KÖY or BEYKOZ. You can reach them all by steamer, which makes a wonderful romantic evening, or take a bus.

THE BOSPHORUS

The Bosphorus, Constantinople's 'Garland of Waters' is one of the most glorious amenities of any city in the world, and the city makes full use of it; every few minutes there is a steamer leaving from the quays at Eminönü, Karaköy or Kabataş, ferrying crowds of commuters or trippers to the towns and villages on the shores of Europe and Asia. For the sheer delight of wind and sea on a hot summer day, hop on a ferry anywhere; it costs only a few lira.

The most regular service crosses to ÜSKÜDAR, 20 minutes away on the Asian side. Here you can see more fine mosques, notably the ISKELE CAMII, the ŞEMSI PAŞA CAMII and the ATIK VALIDE CAMII, all built by Sinan. Just 1 km south of the ferry terminal, is the KARACA AHMET MEZARLIK, the biggest graveyard in the Islamic world; here you can stroll for hours, shaded by a forest of sweet-smelling cypresses. The tomb-stones entwined with grass and weeds are fascinating in themselves. The sex and station in life of the incumbent is shown by the style of the headgear carved on the stone; turban, fez or more elaborate.

Near the graveyard is the enormous SELIMIYE BARRACKS, where Florence Nightingale saved the lives of thousands of wounded soldiers in the Crimean War; there is a small MUSEUM devoted to her in the barracks, but you must get permission from the officer-in-charge to visit. If you are energetic you can climb to the top of ÇAMLICA HILL, about 4 km from the quay, or take bus No 9. This is the highest hill in the area, and from the summit the views are wonderful; on a clear day you can see as far as Ulu Dağı and the Black Sea. If you're not energetic, just sit in the windy square at ÜSKÜDAR İSKELE and look at the city over the water.

The TOWER you pass on the way back was originally a Byzantine fort; a great chain ran from here to the tip of SERAGLIO POINT, by which the mouth of the Bosphorus could be closed. What you see today is an eighteenth-century building, now used as an observation post. Of course there is the usual legend of the Princess and the Snake attached to this tower – hence the name, KIZ KULESI, Maiden's Tower.

You can take a steamer-trip all the way up the Bosphorus and back; this service is known as the *Boğaziçi özel Gezi Seferleri*, and there are four or five departures a day from Terminal 4, by the Galata Bridge. It's a lovely trip, taking about two hours each way, and calling in at most of the ports on the European and Asian shores. If you stay on board all the way to ANADOLU KAVAĞI (which is recommended), you will have 1½ hours to wait in that pretty village with its excellent waterside restaurants, before the steamer leaves. Otherwise you could get off at one of the European villages and take a bus or *dolmuş* back to the city. The big international hotels have their own 'cruise' boats which take you in luxury, but cost a great deal more money.

The first stop on the European shore is BEŞIKTAŞ, for the HAYRETTIN PAŞA or BARBAROSSA NAVAL MUSEUM and for the DOLMABAHÇE PALACE. This extraordinary wedding-cake of a palace was built by Abdül Mecit I in 1847, as he found the Topkapı Sarayı oppressive and confining. He obviously thought the same of traditional Ottoman architecture, for the palace looks uncompromisingly to Europe in its conception and design, rejecting altogether the Ottoman influence. The result, though undeniably impressive, with its immense Baroque façade and jetty, all in white marble, gives the impression of a rather ingenuous and confused attempt at European grandeur. The interior too, is an orgy of magnificent baubles, with innumerable ornaments of incredible opulence, heaped one upon another, with little idea of a unifying whole. It's certainly worth a visit; though, as at the Topkapı harem, you are shepherded round in tightly controlled groups. The palace is still frequently used for State visits and security is paramount. The most impressive rooms in the whole, vast building are probably the sultans' lavish marble bathrooms.

Much more manageable and harmonious, though in a similar European Baroque style, is the pretty little palace of BEYLERBEYI, on the Asian side just north of the great Bosphorus Bridge; the best way to get there is by bus from ÜSKÜDAR.

The Strait is dominated at its narrowest point, 10 km north of the bridge, by the two castles of ANADOLU HISAR and RUMELI HISAR. Rumeli Hisar was built by Mehmet the Conqueror in 1452, to cut Constantinople off from grain supplies and military assistance from the Black Sea. Believe it or not, this huge fortification was built in less than four months, an astounding achievement. Today it has been restored and is used in the summer for open-air theatre and concerts. Across the strait, the Anatolian Castle is much smaller and older, built by Beyazıt I. Nearby is KÜÇÜKSU, the 'Sweet Waters of Asia', which used to be a favourite picnic spot for the Ottoman nobility; it is still delightful, with its pretty fishing village, and the river flowing through meadows into the Bosphorus.

The rest of the Bosphorus is lined with attractive villages, now sadly dwarfed by the proliferation of modern building behind them. Most of these villages have hotels and waterside fish restaurants; a wonderful retreat from the noise and murk of the Great City. The most interesting villages are ARNAVUTKÖY, KANLICA, YENIKÖY and SARIYER. From RUMELI KAVAĞI at the top of the European shore, you can take a taxi or *dolmuş* to KILYOS, a small resort on the Black Sea, with a fine sandy beach.

THE PRINCES' ISLANDS

The other popular steamer destination is out to the Princes' Islands, an hour away to the south-east of the city. Here is a little archipelago of nine islands, four of which are inhabited. Take a boat from the east end of Eminönü Iskele, preferably on a weekday, for the boats are crammed to the gunwales at weekends; your *jeton* in the turnstile entitles you to a return trip to any one of the islands.

For many years the islands were populated by monks, nuns and a few fishermen, for in Byzantine times there were monasteries, convents and churches on all of them. Each island too, even the tiniest, would have tales to tell of Byzantine emperors and empresses, banished from the city to live the rest of their lives in these isolated religious communities. During Ottoman times, the Christian communities disbanded, and the islands reverted to their solitude. In the nineteenth century, interest revived in the islands as a resort and, with the introduction of a regular ferry service, many wealthy Istanbulus moved out here. A number of pretty wooden *Yalıs* from this period remain today; on BÜYÜK ADA, one has been converted to a modest but delightful hotel.

The great feature of the islands today is that there is no motor traffic; transport is by horse-drawn 'Phaeton', an important factor in preserving their quiet charm and limiting the development that so mars the villages of the Bosphorus.

KINALI is the nearest to Istanbul, the smallest of the inhabited islands. Many were the emperors and empresses of Byzantium who ended their years in exile at the old PANAGHIA MONASTERY. The last was Romanus IV Diogenes, who was deposed, exiled and blinded for his poor performance against the Seljuk Turks at the momentous Battle of Manzikert in 1071. Nothing remains of the monastery today; it was utterly destroyed by the guns of the British Admiral Duckworth in 1807, in the belief that a party of Turkish soldiers was hiding there. Kınalı has some good beaches, but it is rather barren and dull.

Next comes BURGAZADA, quiet well-wooded and pretty, with some lovely coves for bathing.

HEYBELIADA has a HOTEL, the Panorama, and dozens of RESTAURANTS, the best of which is the Gazino, out in the pinewoods to the south-west of the town; take a Phaeton, or half-an-hour's stroll. Dominating one of the island's two hills are the grand buildings of the GREEK THEOLOGICAL COLLEGE, built in 1841. Today it is a school, said to contain a major library of Byzantine manuscripts. All around the island are rocky coves and stony beaches for bathing in the cool clear water of the Sea of Marmara.

BÜYÜKADA is the largest of the islands, and the farthest from the city. Crowning the two hills, two MONASTERIES remain, though there were at least four in Byzantine times, as well as a NUNNERY, endowed by the Empress Eirene. Therein lies a story, as told by John Freely:

'In 797, Eirene usurped the throne from her son, Constantine VI, whom she mutilated so badly that he died a few days later. The Emperor left behind a young daughter, the Princess Euphrosyne, whom Eirene banished to a Convent on Prinkipo (as Büyükada was then known), so that she could not contest the throne. In 802 Eirene was herself deposed, and exiled to

Lesbos, where she died shortly afterwards. Her body was taken to Prinkipo, to be buried in the garden of her convent. Euphrosyne remained in the convent for 26 years, while five Emperors in turn succeeded one another on the throne of Byzantium. The last of these ephemeral Emperors, Michael II, the Stammerer, in 829 suddenly grew tired of his old wife, the Empress Thecla, and looked about for a new one. Rumour reached him of the pretty Princess-nun who had been locked up all these years on Prinkipo. So he sent for her, and apparently liked what he saw, for he soon banished Thecla to the convent, and married Euphrosyne. Later that same year, Michael died and was succeeded by his son, Theophilus. The new Emperor showed himself a loyal son, for he restored his mother, Thecla, to the palace, and sent Euphrosyne back to her convent on Prinkipo, where she lived to a ripe old age.'

There are plenty of small HOTELS in the town itself and scattered around the coast among the pinewoods and secluded coves. RESTAURANTS are in great plenty too, for this is a very popular place with Istanbulus, who come here in droves at the weekends. Büyükada would make a good, quiet place to stay while sightseeing in Istanbul; the Express Ferry only takes an hour to the city.

C·H·A·P·T·E·R·4

Ancient and Modern Capitals

Bursa

BURSA is a busy modern industrial city, and at first glance you may wonder why you've bothered to make the effort to visit it. But whereas Istanbul is a glorious hotch-potch of different architectural styles, Bursa scores as a uniquely Turkish city.

The Turks call it *Yeşil Bursa* (Green Bursa); when you start to explore, you'll see why. There are trees everywhere, cypress, plane and mulberry; oases of green in the city. The most famous buildings in Bursa are the YEŞIL CAMI (GREEN MOSQUE) and the YEŞIL TÜRBE (GREEN MAUSOLEUM). Green is the holy colour of Islam, and this city has for centuries been a Moslem stronghold.

The city was originally called Prusia, after its second century BC founder, King Prusias of Bithynia. During the Roman occupation it had the distinction

Detail of Seljuk decoration

of being governed by the famous geographer Pliny the Younger, and later, the Byzantine Emperor, Justinian, built himself a palace and bath complex here, so he could take advantage of Bursa's famous thermal springs.

In spite of Justinian's patronage, Bursa remained little more than a prosperous, but unimportant provincial town, until its proximity to Constantinople, made it a highly desirable prize for successive, would-be conquerors. The Seljuk Turks took the city in 1075, but for nearly 300 years it fell into the hands of one power after another, and there was little opportunity for peaceful development. In 1326 its fortunes started to change. After a siege that lasted for ten long years, instigated by Osman, founder of the Ottoman dynasty, the city finally fell to Osman's son, Orhan. Much taken, as his father had been, with the city, Orhan declared Bursa the capital of what was then no more than a small 'principality' and vigorously set about turning it into a city fit for a sultan. Influenced both by Seljuk and Byzantine architecture, the Ottomans still managed to create a style all their own, and it is from this period onwards that the finest Ottoman religious buildings in Turkey were constructed.

The Ottomans also developed Bursa's silk industry, which still thrives today. This sound economic base stood Bursa in good stead when the rapidly growing Ottoman Empire transferred its capital to Edirne, the better to control the newly-conquered territories in the Balkans. No longer the focus of political activity, but still much favoured by the sultans, the city enjoyed a long period of peaceful prosperity. It suffered a minor hiccup when the Greeks occupied it briefly after the First World War, but in 1922, both the occupying forces and the Greek citizens were expelled by Atatürk and his new Turkish Republic.

You can see pretty well everything of major interest in one very active day, but try and stay overnight if you have time; only this way can you really absorb the atmosphere of this delightful city. It is often touted as a day's excursion from Istanbul, and although this is feasible, you'll spend more time travelling, than in the city itself. If you decide to go it alone from Istanbul, the cheapest and nicest way is to take a ferry to YALOVA and then a bus or a *dolmuş* from Yalova to Bursa.

You could do worse than to start your tour of Bursa with a visit to the TOURIST INFORMATION OFFICE. You'll find it on ATATÜRK CADDESI. It is undoubtedly one of the scruffiest tourist offices in Turkey (or was at the time of writing), but run by the most charming and enthusiastic staff. Here you can pick up a map and advice on where to stay.

From the Tourist Information Office, take a taxi or a *dolmuş* eastwards along ATATÜRK CADDESI to EMIR SULTAN to see the EMIR SULTAN MOSQUE. Built in the 1420s by the daughter of Sultan Beyazıt 'the Thunderbolt', in memory of her husband, it was twice destroyed by earthquakes. Although it has been well restored, it is worth a visit chiefly for its beautiful setting and its view of the city and the valley.

You can walk from here to two of Bursa's main attractions – the YEŞIL CAMI and the YEŞIL TÜRBE. Once again the setting is lovely but this time both the mosque and the tomb are worth visiting in their own right. Some even consider the Yeşil Cami, small though it is, to be the finest mosque in Turkey.

The tomb is the most immediately eye-catching building, but visit the mosque first. If you've forgotten to bring a headscarf, or you are unsuitably dressed, robes and shawls are provided at the entrance.

Sultan Mehmet I had this mosque built in the 1420s, and the stunning, lavishly tiled interior was restored with great care and skill in 1864. The colours are predominantly peacock-blue and the designs reflect the Islamic passion for intricate, geometric patternwork. Note especially the fountain, intricately carved out of one block of marble.The ceiling is beautiful, as is the 15 m high, magnificently tiled *mihrab*. The galleries that surround the main prayer-hall were reserved for the sultan and his harem. In the sultan's private loggia, directly over the main entrance, there is more spectacular tilework.

The Yeşil Türbe is opposite the Yeşil Cami. Here Sultan Mehmet I is buried, together with his children and his nurse. The tiles on the exterior of the tomb are not original; they were added during restoration work in the mid-1800s. The interior, however, is the genuine article, and just as fabulous as that of the mosque. An incongruous, rusty postcard-stand has been injudiciously placed just inside the entrance, but nothing could really reduce the powerful impact of this riot of colour and intricate design.

Just down the road from here is the MUSEUM OF TURKISH AND ISLAMIC ANTIQUITIES housed in a Seljuk *medrese* (theological school). Both the building itself and the exhibits it contains – carpets, weaponry, jewellery and a magnificent collection of handwritten Korans – are well worth a visit.

North-east of the Yeşil complex is the YILDIRIM BEYAZIT CAMII, another *medrese* and the TÜRBE OF SULTAN BEYAZIT 'THE THUNDERBOLT'. Beyazıt earned his impressive nickname before his short reign ended in an ignominious defeat. He succeeded in expanding the Ottoman Empire eastwards and westwards, but eventually came face to face with Tamerlane and was thoroughly defeated in a battle on the outskirts of Ankara in 1402. Tamerlane took great delight in humiliating his captive and Beyazıt died a broken man a year later. These buildings are not in the same league as the Yeşil Camii and Türbe, in terms of elaborate interior decoration, but they were also the victims of earthquakes and, presumably due to lack of funds, were not so lavishly restored.

Take a taxi or *dolmuş* back to ATATÜRK CADDESI and get off near the Tourist Information Office. Take one of the streets running north if you want to explore Bursa's extensive BAZAAR. The original *bedesten* was destroyed by the 1855 earthquake but it's still a fascinating place to spend a few hours. Don't expect the exotica of the Grand Bazaar in Istanbul; this is a 'workaday' market and the locals do their shopping here. If you are patient, and have plenty of time to spare, you are quite likely to find better bargains than anywhere else in Turkey – especially in the copper, brassware and jewellery line.

In between ATATÜRK CADDESI and the Bazaar, is Bursa's

ULU CAMII or Grand Mosque. Beyazit built this one too; it's the largest in the city with 20 small, rounded domes, or cupolas. The interior shows considerably more restraint than the later Yeşil Camii, but the *mihrab* is magnificently elaborate, as is the beautifully carved *minber* or pulpit.

North-west of the Ulu Camii is the oldest mosque in Bursa – the ORHAN CAMII. It was built on the orders of Orhan in 1339 and restored in 1417. It is a simple structure, reflecting the style of Seljuk architecture, and was built before the Ottomans really started to find their own architectural style.

Return to ATATÜRK CADDESI and head westwards towards MURADIYE for the HISAR, or citadel, area. Little remains of the original Ottoman walls, but here you will find some of the oldest, and most picturesque wooden houses in Bursa. Near the CLOCK TOWER are the TOMBS OF ORHAN and OSMAN, the founders of Ottoman Bursa and of the empire that followed. The tombs were completely destroyed in the big earthquake of 1855 but rebuilt in 1863. Osman's tomb has especially attractive, Baroque style, internal decorations.

Walking up the hill in a westerly direction, you will find the Muradiye complex and gardens, built for Sultan Murat II. The complex consists of the MURADIYE CAMII, a *medrese* and a cluster of TOMBS. Murat II ordered that his tomb should not be sealed, so that the sun and the rain could enter and, in accordance with his wishes, an opening was left in the dome. Many of the tombs here are beautifully decorated, especially the CEM TÜRBE and the MUSTAFA ŞEHZADE TÜRBE with its fine tilework.

When you've had your fill of tombs, pay a visit to the nearby EIGHTEENTH CENTURY OTTOMAN HOUSE. It has been very well restored and is now used as a museum.

Bursa's popular KULTUR PARK is west of the city centre. Follow ATATÜRK CADDESI which then becomes ALTIPARMAK CADDESI and finally ÇEKIRGE CADDESI. The park is to the right of this road. Any *dolmuş* marked *Çekirge* will do. The Turks have a particular flair when it comes to parks, and this one is no exception. The setting is splendid, the trees and flowerbeds well-tended and well laid out and there is plenty to amuse everyone. In the park are the ARCHAEOLOGICAL MUSEUM, an artificial LAKE and a sizeable FUN-FAIR. Opposite the Kultur Park is the ATATÜRK MUSEUM. This nineteenth-century house is where Atatürk stayed when he came to visit Bursa, and everything in it has been arranged as it was when he stayed here.

ÇEKIRGE is Bursa's most westerly suburb; it is because of the hot, mineral-rich springs here that the city found such early favour with the Byzantine Emperor Justinian, and later with the Ottoman sultans. It is still popular today and hundreds visit it every year to 'take the waters' in the hope of curing all manner of ailments, particularly those of a rheumatic nature. Hotels, ranging from the very grand, by Turkish standards, to the incredibly cheap and very basic, have their own private baths. If you are not planning to stay overnight in Bursa, you can visit one of the PUBLIC BATHS in the area, but just one soak is unlikely to work miracles for any ailment you might be seeking to cure.

. Bursa's ULU DAĞI (Great Mountain) is Turkey's foremost skiing resort. The area is a National Park and, even out of the skiing season, it's a wonderful place to enjoy the cool, mountain air amongst the pine-forests. By car it's about 35 km south-east of the city, or you can take the FUNICULAR RAILWAY.

EDIRNE

In the year 1025, the Roman Emperor Hadrian founded the city of Hadrianopolis on the site of today's EDIRNE. The city has always been an important military outpost, fortified as it is by the loop in the River Tunca; under the Byzantines, it was a bastion against the Barbarians of northern Europe; the Ottomans used it as a springboard for their western expansion, and today it is a buttress against neighbouring Greece. In 1362 Sultan Murat, taking advantage of the strife between Latin and Greek Christians, which had nearly brought the Byzantine Empire to its knees, walked with his army through the gates of the city, thus completing his conquest of Thrace. The Ottoman capital was moved from Bursa to Edirne, which now became the centre of operations. After 1453 the capital was again moved, this time to Constantinople, but Edirne continued to thrive as an important and richly endowed city.

Today it is a pleasant little town, the capital of agricultural Thrace; it has little industry; its main reason for existence is as the first Turkish town on the main road from Europe. It's hard to imagine it as the great capital of the early Ottoman Empire, but it does possess some of Turkey's finest and most important Ottoman monuments.

Even if you're not an enthusiastic and knowledgeable connoisseur of mosques, it's not hard to appreciate the magnificence of the three principal mosques of Edirne. The most celebrated is the SELIMIYE, the culmination of the career of Sinan, whom you cannot fail to have run into, as the greatest architect of the Ottoman Empire. Sinan was over 80 in 1575, when he built this mosque; he said of it, 'Shehzade Mosque was my apprenticeship; the Süleymaniye my journeyman's work; and the Selimiye at Edirne, my masterpiece.'

Immense and towering over the town, it is certainly the finest mosque in Turkey. As you enter the main door, you see the great dome soaring above on its eight massive piers; beneath is a richly carpeted ocean of peace and space. You, yourself, fill such a tiny speck of this immensity, that you cannot help but feel a greater presence. The marble courtyard and cloisters are simple, and instead of cluttering it all up, they guide the eye and the concentration to the perfect harmony of the dome, half-domes and minarets. The main dome itself finally fulfilled the dream of Ottoman architects, to surpass the great dome of Aghia Sofia in Istanbul; (see the section on Istanbul, and Architecture). The Selimiye's dome has a span of 33 m, an incredible architectural achievement. It is made all the more remarkable by Sinan's decision to dispense with the semi-domes which, under normal circumstances, would buttress against the enormous forces exerted by the main dome. The interior decoration again is simple and uncluttered; the effect comes from the interplay of light and space. The slender minarets at each corner are 71 m high, the perfect counterpoint to the massive leaden dome.

Right in the centre of town is the ESKI CAMII, a completely different kettle of fish. This mosque was built for Mehmet I, 170 years before the Selimiye, in the early years of the Ottoman Empire. It has one minaret, quite enough for the *Muezzin* to climb and call the faithful to prayer. Similar in form to the Ulu Camii at Bursa, it has no great dome, but a sensible arrangement of nine smaller domes on four massive rectangular piers. It's a solid, earthy, no-nonsense mosque. It's distinctive for the Koranic scriptures painted directly onto both the outside and inside walls, or fired onto tiles. Calligraphy, in Ottoman times, was a highly regarded art form; the Eski Camii has some of Turkey's finest examples.

The other famous mosque is the ÜÇ ŞEREFELI

Uç Şerefeli minaret

CAMII, built in the mid-fifteenth century for Murad II. This is one of the earliest mosques with a distinctly Ottoman style, a pointer to the refinements to come. The dome, 24 m across, is an early attempt at emulating Aghia Sofia. The tall, graceful minarets were used for the first time in this mosque.

Near the Üç Şerefeli is the SOKULLU MEHMET PAŞA HAMAM. Here, you have the opportunity to bathe in a *Hamam* designed by Sinan himself; combining the delights of the Turkish Bath with the enjoyment of wonderful architecture. The baths have recently been restored and overhauled.

There are two fine covered markets in Edirne; the one attached to the Eski Camii, the ALI PAŞA ÇARŞISI, was designed by Sinan. The architecture is more interesting than the wares on sale; the same is true of the KAVAFLAR ARASTA attached to the Selimiye.

Down the hill is the RIVER TUNCA; there is a peaceful poplar-lined track along the bank. Here are a number of graceful Ottoman bridges, the oldest of which is the beautiful six-arched BEYAZIT KÖPRÜ at the bottom of VILAYET CADDESI; cross the bridge for the BEYAZIT II MOSQUE AND HOSPITAL. Built in 1484, this complex reverts to a simpler theme than the earlier Üç Şerefeli; the simple dome of the prayer-hall, plonked squarely on the cube of its walls, is the fundamental principle of all Ottoman architecture. Two unadorned minarets rise from the complex of smaller domed buildings surrounding the prayer-hall. The cloisters surrounding the courtyard, which here, is laid to lawn, use old Byzantine marble pillars, for the Ottomans never got the knack of fashioning these perfect columns. As well as a religious school and a kitchen for the poor, the complex contained what is said to be the world's first mental hospital. (London's Bedlam Hospital, such as it was, was founded in 1547.) In the great hall of the asylum is a fountain and a daïs where the resident orchestra of ten musicians would play to calm and distract psychopathic and melancholy patients. Evliya Efendi, a contemporary writer, notes, 'they have excellent food twice a day; even pheasants, partridges and other birds are supplied'. This early humane treatment of the insane, undoubtedly stems from the Islamic belief that the insane are 'Touched by the Hand of God'. Currently the complex is being restored. It's set in a garden on a grassy bank of the river; very few people visit it, so you can usually have it all to yourself, and it's well worth it.

· Apart from the gems of Ottoman architecture dotted about the town, it's worth just strolling around Edirne; there are many elegant Ottoman houses, seriously dilapidated, and the usual lively street-life of a Turkish town. The best RESTAURANTS are around the main square, off TALAT PAŞA CADDESI – near the Tourist Information Office. There are a couple of good HOTELS in the town, and a great number of cheaper PANSIYONS.

The best time to visit Edirne would be in the second week of June, for this is when the famous GREASED WRESTLING MATCHES take place at KIRKPINAR. This is one of Turkey's most celebrated sporting events, and contestants gather from all parts of the country to smear their huge bodies with olive oil and slither into lubricious combat. Edirne makes the most of this and puts on a host of festivities, with folk-dancing, music, exhibitions, fairs and markets and goodness knows what else.

All this can be enjoyed on the way into Turkey, or at the end of a four hour bus-ride from Istanbul. The buses are cheap and very frequent.

ANKARA

When the Ottoman Empire finally crumbled after the First World War and Mustafa Kemal Atatürk formed the new Turkish Republic he declared the small, unimportant town of ANKARA its capital. The population was then a mere 40,000; today, it is over 3 million and growing fast, as Turks from outlying rural areas crowd into the city, in search of a better life.

Atatürk's 'brave new city' is the governmental and political hub of the Turkish Republic and the pulse of modern Turkey. But it has none of Istanbul's atmosphere of faded grandeur, nor can it compete with the sophisticated cultural melting pot of the former capital. Ankara is brash, energetic, fast-moving, and probably very exciting to those who enjoy the vitality of a modern city.

If you are spending a long time in Turkey, you should certainly visit Ankara; otherwise, it shouldn't be a high priority, unless you have a specific interest in the HITTITE CIVILI-SATION. Ankara's ARCHAEOLOGICAL MUSEUM has a wonderful collection of Hittite artefacts, and the city itself is quite convenient for visiting the ruins of ancient Hittite cities, such as BOĞAZKALE or ALACAHÖYÜK, although the best, HATTUŞAŞ, is about 200 km away.

There are plenty of good HOTELS, although they are expensive by Turkish standards; there are also modern SHOPS and excellent RESTAURANTS in every price range.

Ankara didn't begin with Atatürk; there were settlements on this spot as far back as 1500 BC. The town's fortunes were governed by its position near the centre of the vast Anatolian plateau. It prospered as a stopping-off point on major trade

Hittite artefacts

routes, but suffered the attentions of successive conquerors, from Alexander the Great to Tamerlane, as they passed this way.

The first settlers are thought to have been the Hittites. Little was known of these people until quite recently, but it would seem that their civilisation rivalled that of the ancient Egyptians, and indeed, examples of their art on display in the Ankara Archaeological Museum bear this out. The Phrygians ruled Ankara next, taking over from the Hittites around 1000 BC. Alexander the Great took the city, after a short period of Persian domination and, following his death, Ankara was governed by one of his generals, Seleucus. Meanwhile tribes from Gaul were being imported to Anatolia by the King of Bithynia, in order to beef up his army, and they eventually settled here. They didn't spend much time in the area, as they were too busy bullying other cities, especially in the south-west, into paying them unjustifiable tributes. Eventually Ankara, then known as Ankyra, was annexed to Rome in 25 BC, and the Emperor Augustus set about developing the city, although the administration was left in the hands of the Gauls.

Ankara fared quite well under Roman and Byzantine rule, although it was conquered and held for brief periods by the Arabs and the Persians. The Seljuks held the city with difficulty, and the great Ottoman Sultan, Beyazıt, met his nemesis, in the form of Tamerlane, in a bloody battle just outside Ankara.

Make for the CITADEL first. At the top are the crumbling remains of the BYZANTINE FORTIFICATIONS and within the walls a cluster of old and ramshackle TURKISH HOUSES. You can get some idea of the scale of the city from here. Back down the hill is the ARCHAEOLOGICAL MUSEUM, partially housed in a magnificent old *bedesten*, thought to have been constructed in 1471. Before you go into the museum, take a look at some of the Hittite statues which decorate the museum gardens. It is not a very large museum, but it is superbly laid out and the exhibits are well labelled and displayed. Even if museums leave you cold, you are unlikely to remain unmoved by this one. The 'completeness' of so many of the exhibits, many over 7,000 years old, is astounding.

Finds from the prehistoric Palaeolithic (stone-age), Neolithic (new stone-age) and Chalcolithic (stone and copper age) periods are found in the rooms to the right as you enter the museum. The next part of the museum is devoted to the Hittites (Bronze Age). Beautiful pottery, finely worked gold jewellery and miniature statuary are amongst the most impressive exhibits.

When the Hittite Empire declined, various smaller kingdoms took control of parts of Anatolia during the 800 or so years before the birth of Christ. The Phrygians, whose most famous ruler was King Midas of Golden Touch fame, established themselves in the Ankara region, with their capital city at Gordion; the museum has an excellent collection of Phrygian artefacts including huge, elaborately decorated cauldrons. Much further to the east, the Urartians, about whom little is known, had set up shop in the area of Lake Van; ivory, gold and silver ornaments are the most interesting objects in the finest collection of Urartian artefacts in the world.

The final rooms of the museum are devoted to the Classical Greek and Roman periods. In the Central Hall are some of the monumental finds from various archaeological sites all over the country. Most of these date from the Hittite period.

Down from the citadel hill, to the south-east, you will find Ankara's BAZAAR and a cluster of MOSQUES including the Seljuk ARSLANHANE CAMII, constructed at the end of the thirteenth century from the remains of Roman and Byzantine buildings. Note the superbly carved wooden *minber*.

What little remains of Roman Ankara can be seen to the north-west of the citadel. The COLUMN OF JULIAN is located in HÜKÜMET MEYDANI. It was built in the middle of the fourth century to commemorate the visit of the Emperor Julian to the city. Julian was noted for restoring the pagan practices of the pre-Christian empire, and was obviously welcomed by the

Galatians who, as we know from St Paul's stern letters, weren't exactly model Christians. Nowadays, a stork is occasionally to be seen, triumphantly in residence at the top of the 17 m high column.

North of the column is Ankara's most well-attended mosque, the HACI BAYRAM CAMII. On a Friday, especially during Ramazan, the faithful spill out of the mosque into the square and the surrounding streets. They use polythene sheets or newspapers as makeshift prayer mats. The mosque, built in the fifteenth century, is dedicated to the founder of an order of Dervishes who were based in Ankara.

Immediately adjoining the mosque are the rather disappointing remains of the TEMPLE OF AUGUSTUS. The temple, built around 200 BC, was originally dedicated to the Phrygian Moon God, and then to the fertility goddess, Cybele. When the Roman emperors decided to deify themselves, the temple was re-dedicated to Augustus. The Byzantines turned it into a church.

To the west of the Temple of Augustus are the remains of the ROMAN BATHS built by the Emperor Caracalla in the early part of the third century. Nothing more than the ruined lower walls remain, but you can work out the general pattern of the baths with their separate groups of rooms; frigidarium (cold rooms), which would have included a plunge pool, the tepidarium (warm rooms) and the caldarium (hot rooms) where bathers would sweat it out in the forerunner of the Turkish Bath. You can still see the remains of the elaborate heating system that serviced the complex.

You cannot visit Ankara without seeing the MAUSOLEUM OF ATATÜRK. If you had any doubt as to the place this extraordinary man holds in the hearts of the Turkish people, you won't after you've seen the monumental tomb that took nearly ten years to build.

Whatever you may think of this neo-Classical building, nobody can deny that it's impressive. At the start of the splendid marble-paved approach avenue, are two kiosks. One holds a model of the tomb itself, together with architectural plans and photographs taken during its construction. The avenue is flanked by statues of Hittite Lions and lush, precisely manicured vegetation.

The mausoleum complex houses the tomb of Atatürk's successor, Ismet İnönü. There are also museums containing all manner of Atatürk's possessions; from the simplest item of clothing to his collection of private and official limousines. There are lavish gifts bestowed on Atatürk by contemporary world leaders, and portrait after portrait of Atatürk posed with this prime minister, or that king. His library collection is most impressive, although one wonders when this incredibly vigorous man ever had time to read.

Atatürk's mausoleum in Ankara

The mausoleum proper is approached by a stairway whose proportions show a proper sense of occasion. On either side of the huge entrance doors, carved into the walls, are extracts from Atatürk's famous speech on the occasion of the tenth anniversary of the republic, and known as the 'Testament to Youth'. Inside, the vast hall is faced with marble and decorated with gilded mosaics. Atatürk's tomb stands in splendid isolation, carved from one huge piece of marble, at the end of the hall.

C·H·A·P·T·E·R· 5

The Aegean Coast

ÇANAKKALE

There are two good reasons for including ÇANAKKALE on your itinerary. Firstly, as a base for visiting TROY (27 km away) and, secondly, to see Gallipoli, the site of one of the bloodiest battles of the First World War, in which thousands of Australians, New Zealanders, British and Turks lost their lives. For hundreds of young Australians and New Zealanders, a visit to the GALLIPOLI Peninsula, directly across the Dardanelles from Çanakkale, is an obligatory pilgrimage.

Take a look at the map and you will see why the area is of such strategic importance. During the First World War the Turks, allied with Imperial Germany, effectively bottled up Russia with their control of the straits. Churchill, hoping to put the Ottoman Empire out of the game right at the outset of war, and open up the Black Sea route through the

Dardanelles to the Russians, threw the might of the Allied fleet into the straits. The Turks, in spite of outmoded defence systems, held strong, and on 25 April 1915, after heavy naval losses, the Allies gave up and decided to try their luck on land. Disembarking on the Gallipoli Peninsula they were met with fierce resistance from the Turkish forces, particularly from a division led by Mustafa Kemal Atatürk. After nine months of sporadically heavy fighting, the Allies withdrew from Gallipoli.

MEMORIALS, CEMETERIES and MONUMENTS to British, French, Turkish, Australian and New Zealand soldiers can be found all over the area. Look to the hills of the Gallipoli Peninsula and you can read these words:

Stop O passer by
This Earth you tread unawares
Once witnessed the end of an Era.
Bow and listen! This quiet mound
Is where the heart of a nation throbs

TROY

If you visit TROY (Truva) anticipating spectacular ruins you will be disappointed. Troy offers not so much ruins, as ruined ruins. Only those with a knowledge of archaeology are likely to be able to make any sense out of the haphazard network of walls, mounds, trenches and stone blocks, which is all that remains of the city. There is a rather grotesque WOODEN HORSE at the entrance to the site, used mainly as an 'adventure playground' for children, and if you visit the scruffy souvenir shop which doubles as a cafe, you will see that someone with a sense of humour has nailed a pair of shoes to the door jamb. One shoe has a hole in the heel and is daubed with red paint!

But, if you are blessed with a little imagination and you refresh your memory with the story of the Trojan war, it is a wonderfully evocative place and the surrounding countryside, especially in the spring, is quite beautiful.

Troy was a romantic invention, a product of Homer's brilliant imagination. Neither the Trojan War, nor the rich cast of characters involved, nor even the city itself, actually existed – this was the belief held by the academic community right up to the nineteenth century. There were always incurable romantics who had believed that Homer's *Iliad* was at least based on fact, but none of them was ever taken seriously.

Scant attention was paid by academics to a book by a certain Charles McClaren, which took all the topographical references given by Homer in his poem, and matched them to the area surrounding the MOUND OF HISARLIK. Little more credence was given to the findings of Frank Calvert, an Englishman who actually owned part of the mound and had carried out some preliminary diggings. Enter, in 1868, Heinrich Schliemann, a former grocer, but now a wealthy, self-taught, amateur archaeologist with a passionate belief in the existence of Homer's Troy.

Under the sceptical and disparaging nose of the academic community, Schliemann obtained the necessary permission from the Ottoman government and started, at his own expense, to dig. He discovered fairly quickly that he had undertaken rather more than he had anticipated. Schliemann's excavations, haphazard and unscientific by today's careful standards, started to reveal not one city of Troy, but a whole series, one built on top of the other – a total of nine in all.

Although there is still dispute, it is generally believed that Level IV is that of Homer's Troy. But Schliemann discovered a cache of FABULOUS JEWELS in the strata of Troy II, which convinced him that this was Homer's Troy and the jewels part of the treasure of King Priam. Reluctant to hand over any of his remarkable find to the Turkish authorities, Schliemann, together with his Greek wife Sophia, gave their army of Turkish workers an unexpected day off. Then, they surreptitiously unearthed the treasure which only they had set eyes on, packed it into the folds of Sophia's clothes and successfully smuggled their stupendous find out of Turkey, right under the noses of the Turkish authorities.

It is said that Sophia was to be seen wearing some of the jewels at social gatherings in Athens. The jewels finally found their way to Berlin and disappeared when the Russians entered the city at the end of the Second World War.

The legend of Troy Paris was the son of King Priam of Troy, but at his birth it was foretold that he would bring about the downfall of the city. He was promptly abandoned on Mount Ida to die. Destiny intervened and Paris was rescued by shepherds who raised him to manhood.

Meanwhile, on Mount Olympus, a marriage banquet had been arranged, to which all the gods and goddesses had been invited – all except one – Eris, the Goddess of Discord. With nose much out of joint Eris lived up to her name and threw a golden apple into the banquet, inscribed with the words – 'To the most fair'. After non-starters and minor goddesses had been eliminated, only three ladies were in the running – Aphrodite, Hera and Athena. Zeus, unwilling to become involved in the dispute, packed the three goddesses off to Mount Ida where

The wooden horse at Troy

Paris, who enjoyed a reputation as a connoisseur of women, was designated to be the final arbiter.

All three goddesses decided to hedge their bets and each secretly offered Paris a reward should he choose them. Hera promised him wealth, Athena, wisdom and Aphrodite, the love of the most beautiful woman in the world. Paris promptly awarded the apple to Aphrodite and the first step in the downfall of Troy was taken.

Menelaus, the brother of the powerful Greek King Agamemnon, had recently married the much sought after Helen, considered to be the most beautiful woman in the world. Aphrodite, true to her word, led Paris to the court of Menelaus, where he seduced Helen and carted her off to Troy. Agamemnon and Menelaus, with the help of anyone who was anyone in Greece, prepared a vast fleet of 1,000 black ships and set sail for Troy seeking vengeance. Thus began the Trojan War.

In the course of the war Hector, another son of King Priam, was killed by the great Achilles, who was himself eventually slain by Paris, with a well-aimed arrow to the vulnerable heel; for Achilles' mother, grasping him by the foot, as she immersed him as a baby in the magical waters of the River Styx, had neglected to soak his heel.

To make matters worse the gods and goddesses took a special interest in the war, with the two 'beauty contest' also-rans, Hera and Athena, intervening for the Greeks whenever the fancy took them. For ten long years the war raged on until finally, a devious but simple plan was devised by the Greek King Odysseus. The Greeks seemingly withdrew, anchoring their fleet in a secluded bay just out of sight of Troy. They left behind a vast wooden horse as an 'offering to the Gods'. The Trojans, overjoyed at their victory, ignored the warnings of their priest – 'beware Greeks bearing gifts', and, opening their city gates, dragged the horse inside.

In the dead of night, when Troy was sleeping off the victory celebrations, a handful of Greeks secreted in the belly of the horse crept out and opened the city gates to their colleagues. Troy was put to the sword and the torch and within hours nothing remained but ruins.

PERGAMUM

If you are touring in the Aegean region, or based there, you will be spoilt for choice of ruined ancient cities to see. But PERGAMUM is one of the most impressive and a good choice even if you have no informed interest in archaeology.

If you haven't got a car you'll need to do a lot of walking to do the site justice, but you can arrange for a taxi tour from the town of BERGAMA up to the top of the ACROPOLIS and to the ASCLEPION.

When Alexander the Great died, his vast empire was dismembered by his generals, who fought for every last scrap of territory. One of them, Lysimachus, having amassed a huge fortune in plunder, chose to deposit it in the care of his commander, Philetarus in the town of Pergamum. Off to war again, Lysimachus was killed, whereupon Philetarus promptly appropriated the treasure, declaring himself Governor of Pergamum. Thus he became the founder of a dynasty, known as the ATTALIDS. This dynasty was to transform Pergamum from an unimportant backwater into a major power.

Philetarus resisted the temptation to squander his unexpected fortune, and instead, set about currying favour with neighbouring cities and expanding Pergamum itself. His adopted son Eumenes carried on in much the same fashion. His successor, Attalus, another adopted son, was a rather more flamboyant character. Declaring himself king (Philetarus and Eumenes had resisted that temptation), Attalus set about expanding his territory. He was famous for his victory over the Gauls and for the trick he played on his weak-kneed army to get them to fight these ferocious barbarians. The Gauls had been imported by the King of Bithynia to add backbone to his own army and had been allowed to settle in central Asia Minor. From here they made a thorough nuisance of themselves, attacking cities whose governors refused to pay them a tribute. Most paid up, including Attalus, until he decided that enough was enough. Before leading his terrified army into battle, Attalus ordered a sacrifice to the gods. In full view of his men, he plunged his hand into the entrails and displayed the dripping liver, which miraculously bore the words, 'Victory for the King'. Considerably heartened, the army hurled themselves into battle and soundly thrashed the Gauls. Their courage might have been somewhat diminished had they known that Attalus had written the words backwards in ink on his hand, and pressed it against the liver, before presenting this auspicious 'omen'.

Both Attalus and Eumenes II, his successor, knew which horse to back, and consistently curried favour with Rome. This policy paid immense dividends; when the Romans defeated Antiochus the Great of Syria, they decided they didn't want the responsibility of governing the newly conquered lands and handed them over to Pergamum. Overnight the small kingdom found itself in control of a vast territory to the east, as far as Konya in central Anatolia and along the coast as far as Antalya. Eumenes used his new found wealth to transform the city with sumptuous buildings. Intellectual and cultural activities were encouraged and Eumenes, who had a mania for books, set up a library at Pergamum containing over 200,000 of them. Certain sources claim that his hunger for books was so great that his officials commissioned forgeries, just to keep him quiet.

The only library in the world to touch that at Pergamum was at Alexandria, and the Egyptians, fearful that the Pergamum library might one day outshine their own, spitefully cut off the supply of papyrus. Undaunted, Eumenes looked for an alternative and came up with parchment, a writing surface made from dried animal skins. This discovery marked the change from scroll books to the 'Codex' system. Parchment, being brittle, could not be rolled, and the necessity of keeping it flat, resulted in the development of the type of books we know today.

Egypt eventually had the last laugh when Mark Antony raided the library at Pergamum and carried off the best of the collection, as a present for Cleopatra, whose Alexandria library had been destroyed by fire.

Eumenes' successor, Attalus II, carried on the policy of kow-towing to the Romans. He was followed by the last of the Attalids, Attalus III. Not the stuff of which his predecessors were made, Attalus III was an oddball. He spent a good deal of his time absorbed in the study of poisonous plants, from which he developed noxious infusions; these he tested on a regular supply of condemned criminals. He died, childless, after a short and, not surprisingly, unpopular reign, willing his entire kingdom to Rome in recognition, perhaps, of the inevitable.

Pergamum resisted when the Romans came to claim their inheritance, but their efforts were short lived. Although Pergamum remained a free city, the kingdom itself was swallowed up and became the Roman 'Province of Asia'.

Go up to the ACROPOLIS first, where you can get your bearings and enjoy the spectacular view. The palaces of the Attalid kings are now only so much rubble, but German financed restoration work is currently being carried out on the famous LIBRARY of Eumenes II, adjoining the foundations of what used to be a TEMPLE TO ATHENA, the Goddess of Wisdom. The 10,000 seat THEATRE, built into the hillside, is awe-inspiring. At the northern end of the narrow terrace surrounding the theatre, are the remains of a TEMPLE TO DIONYSUS, the God of wine, revelry and all-round good fun.

The foundations of the ALTAR OF ZEUS lie a little to the south of the theatre. Built by Eumenes II, in celebration of his predecessor's spectacular victory over the Gauls, it is considered to be one of the finest achievements of Hellenistic art. But, if you want to see it, you'll have to go to Berlin where, reconstructed, it takes pride of place in the Pergamum Museum.

Down the hill from the Altar of Zeus, between the UPPER and LOWER AGORAS, can be found the ruins of the SANCTUARY OF DEMETER, the GYMNASIUM and the ROMAN BATHS.

Returning to Bergama, take a taxi to the site of the ASCLEPION. An Asclepion was an ancient version of a health clinic; the one at Pergamum was one of the finest in the world. Patients, with all manner of ailments, came from every corner of the civilised world to be cured by the doctor-priests who administered the cult of the God Asclepius and his granddaughters, Hygeia and Panacea.

All were welcome. From what can be pieced together, it would seem that many of the cures were based on sound commonsense, and utilised techniques recognised as viable today. Herbal medicines, massage, dream-therapy, dietary regimes, hot, cold and mud baths and exercise, were all prescribed, with a high degree of success.

You approach the Asclepion by the SACRED WAY; to the right can be seen the remains of the LIBRARY, provided for the edification of the patients. To the left are the scant, circular remains of the most sacred part of the complex, the TEMPLE OF ZEUS-ASCLEPIUS. Beside this are the impressive remains of another round structure, which has never been properly identified. Basins for washing in the sacred water, an essential part of the cure, can still be seen. From here a TUNNEL connects with the SACRED WELL in the centre of the sanctuary. Apparently patients were made to walk down this tunnel alone, while priests whispered reassurances of their eventual cure through holes in the roof!

To the right of the Sacred Well is the THEATRE, where entertainment was regularly provided for the long-stay patients. It has been restored and is often used for performances today.

In Bergama itself, you can visit the ARCHAEOLOGICAL MUSEUM. Indeed it is worth stopping there before you look at the ruins, as many of the finds at Pergamum are displayed here, together with a model of the Altar of Zeus, which will help you put things in perspective as you go round.

In Bergama, you can also see the KIZIL AVLU or 'Red Courtyard'. Built in 200 AD as a temple dedicated to an Egyptian god, the Byzantines adapted it for use as a church.

Izmir

Hunting on the slopes of Mount Pagus, Alexander the Great, overcome with weariness, took a short nap. While he was sleeping, the Goddess Nemesis appeared to him, and instructed him to build a city on that very spot. Alexander met his untimely death before he could carry out the goddess' wishes, and the task of building SMYRNA, the ancient name for Izmir, fell to one of his three heirs, General Lysimachus.

Aeolian and Ionian Greeks had discovered the spot long before Alexander arrived, but they had chosen a site further east, along the beautiful bay of Izmir for their settlement, calling it Bayrakh. Never of much consequence, aside from its claim to be the BIRTHPLACE OF HOMER, the populace were resettled when Lysimachus had finished his work.

Smyrna was successively governed by Rome, Byzantium, the Seljuks and eventually the Ottoman Turks. It suffered numerous earthquakes and was doggedly rebuilt. It was a major battlefield during the Crusades, caught between the forces of Islam and Christianity, and it was put to the sword by the bloodthirsty and monstrously destructive Mongol conqueror, Tamerlane.

Under Ottoman rule things began to look up. The existing Greek population was joined by a large contingent of Jews, fleeing from persecution in Spain. They were welcomed by the

Ottomans, who tolerated a high degree of religious freedom. English, French and Dutch merchants were encouraged to settle in Izmir, and the city became sophisticated and cosmopolitan, with its prosperity rooted in the flourishing tobacco trade. Even two devastating earthquakes at the end of the seventeenth and eighteenth centuries, failed to crush the spirit of the populace.

At the end of the First World War, the Allies prepared to carve up the Ottoman Empire between them. Greece had always had designs on Smyrna and beyond, and following the Treaty of Sèvres, signed between the Allies and the tottering Ottoman government, the Greeks moved in, basing themselves in Smyrna and advancing inland towards Ankara. Their occupation was short lived; Kemal Atatürk's army successfully halted the Greek advance and drove them back to Smyrna. On 9 September 1922 a bloody battle in the city ended in a defeat for the Greeks, a wholesale massacre of the population, a terrible fire that broke out during the last stages of the fighting – and the end of an era. From the ashes yet another new city was built. It was called by its Turkish name – Izmir.

After such a history of fire, earthquakes, conquest and reconquest, it's hardly surprising that today there is little to see that bears witness to former Smyrna's turbulent past. In fact, all the sights worth seeing can be visited in half a day. But Izmir is a fine modern city, with wide, palm-tree lined boulevards and solidly built office and apartment blocks, which are suprisingly easy on the eye. A breeze, known as the *Imbat* obligingly blows up from the Bay of Izmir every afternoon, and fans the city in the height of summer. The citizens of Izmir are very proud of their city, and with good reason.

You can take a *dolmuş* from KONAK MEYDANI, Izmir's main square, to the KADIFEKALE, or Velvet Castle. It was here that Alexander received his instructions from the Goddess Nemesis, and the original acropolis of Smyrna was first built. There are superb views of the city and the bay, and ruins of BYZANTINE and OTTOMAN FORTIFICATIONS.

Returning to Konak Meydanı, take a look at the small, eighteenth century MOSQUE, and at Izmir's elaborate nineteenth century Ottoman CLOCK TOWER; from here you can visit the BAZAAR. Lacking somewhat in exotic Oriental atmosphere, it is, nonetheless, one of the few areas of the city that partially escaped the terrible 1922 fire. The maze of narrow streets teems with activity.

From today's bazaar, step back some 2,000 years and look at the ruins of ancient Smyrna's AGORA, which can be found nearby. Three STATUES, Poseidon, Demeter and Artemis were found during excavations and are displayed, well restored, if a little incomplete.

In CUMHURIYET MEYDANI, north along the waterfront from Konak Meydanı, is an equestrian STATUE of Atatürk, and east of the square along a wide boulevard is the delightful KULTUR PARKI with its artificial lake. Within the confines of the park is the ARCHAEOLOGICAL MUSEUM, displaying extensive finds from the Aegean region. It is worth a visit, especially if you are planning a tour of the ancient sites later in your stay.

There are plenty of good RESTAURANTS in Izmir, but the nicest are to be found on the waterfront between Konak and Cumhuriyet squares. Tables outside overlook the bay and, if your view isn't obscured by a rusty old cargo ship, it's a wonderful place to sip an aperitif before dinner, watching the sun go down over the bay. For cheaper food, and lots of atmosphere, go into the bazaar where you will find plenty of choice hidden away in the narrow streets. Most of these places won't serve alcohol.

If you are planning to visit the major Classical sites in the Aegean and inland, and you don't want to stay in a holiday resort, Izmir is a good alternative base. From here you can reach Ephesus, Miletus, Didyma and Priene to the east, Sardis, Aphrodisias and Pamukkale inland (although an overnight stay at Pamukkale is recommended) and Pergamum to the west. A visit to Troy is also possible, but would make for a very long day.

EPHESUS AND SELÇUK

The ancient city of EPHESUS is one of the most impressive sights in Turkey and if you stir from the beach for nothing else, this is a must. Unfortunately thousands of other tourists think so too. It's rare to find the site not overrun with enthusiastic, noisy tourists; in high season, the multi-tongued babble of the guides and their charges does rather detract from the atmosphere. If you really want to see Ephesus at its best, go alone. Choose the extremes of the day (it's best to avoid the hottest time anyway) or go in the winter.

The site can be reached easily from Kuşadasi by *dolmuş*, or from Izmir by bus. Tour companies arrange visits from Bodrum and Marmaris and you can travel to Ephesus from both these resorts by bus via the nearby town of Selçuk.

The greatness of Ephesus was due to the happy choice of its principal deity and its geographical position; its eventual decline was due to Mother Nature and the coming of Christianity.

The earth-mother goddess, Cybele

When Ionian colonists arrived in Ephesus from Greece, it was already a sacred centre for the cult of Cybele, the Anatolian earth-mother goddess. The indigenous population seem to have accepted the newcomers quite happily, and before long Cybele evolved into Artemis, the Greek goddess of chastity – although the Ephesians seem to have taken a fair degree of licence with the chastity angle.

Ephesus, well situated in the middle of the west coast of Asia Minor, became a prosperous trading centre and the destination of hundreds of pilgrims who came to visit the TEMPLE OF ARTEMIS, one of the Seven Wonders of the Ancient World.

In spite of conquest by the northern Kingdom of Lydia and subsequently, in 546 BC, invasion by the Persians, the city continued to flourish. The Temple of Artemis had been destroyed by fire, but elaborate building plans were put in motion and, when Alexander the Great arrived, driving the Persians out in 334 BC, the temple was nearly completed. He was so impressed by what he saw that he offered to pay for the building costs. The Ephesians, quite wealthy enough to pay themselves, tactfully declined on the grounds that it would not be proper for one god to make a dedication to another.

After Alexander's death and the division of his empire between his generals, Ephesus came under the aegis of Lysimachus. It was now that the city's real enemy started to be bothersome. Silt, deposited by the River Maeander, was causing problems in the harbour; so, Lysimachus had the city rebuilt on its present site, where it was hoped that the new harbour would remain clear.

Amphitheatre

When the Roman Empire swallowed up Anatolia, Ephesus started to enjoy greater prosperity than ever before. The Romans identified Artemis with their own virgin-huntress goddess, Diana, and the already powerful cult, grew ever more influential. Local craftsmen made fortunes out of a brisk business in little statuettes of Artemis/Diana and the city held lavish festivals in celebration of the goddess, attracting visitors, and money, from all over the known world.

But all the while the menace of deposits from the River Maeander were threatening the new harbour, and another equally deadly threat to the prosperity of Ephesus, had begun to make itself felt. St John the Apostle had settled in the area of Ephesus some time after the death of Christ, and many believe that he brought the Virgin Mary with him to live out her days free from persecution. He succeeded in converting a number of Ephesians, no easy task in the face of such a powerful cult as that of Artemis. By the time St Paul arrived in 53 AD there were already a small number of converted to preach to, and with great vigour he set about expanding the congregation. For three years he made considerable progress in Ephesus and eventually succeeded in putting the noses of the craftsmen, who saw their livelihood threatened, thoroughly out of joint. With the battle cry of 'great is Diana of the Ephesians' the craftsmen, led by a certain silversmith called Demetrius, started a riot. Paul was unhurt, but nonetheless, chose to leave the city soon afterwards.

But the seeds were more than sown. Christianity took strong root in Ephesus, and when it became the official state religion, the Temple of Artemis was destroyed. By the sixth century, the harbour had become completely unnavigable, the trading vessels that once visited Ephesus switched to the port of Smyrna, and the city was all but abandoned. Today, Ephesus is over 5 km from the sea.

Excavation and restoration work still continues at Ephesus and much has already been accomplished. It is one of the largest archaeological sites in the world and certainly one of the most 'complete'. Even the uninitiated, where archaeology is concerned, cannot fail to be amazed by it.

To do the site justice you should allow a full day, allowing for a long lunch-break to give your feet a rest. There are four separate areas to visit. The main city itself, the HOUSE OF THE VIRGIN MARY, the GROTTO OF THE SEVEN SLEEPERS and the SITE OF THE TEMPLE OF ARTEMIS. If you are short of time, confine yourself to the city.

From the Selçuk to Kuşadasi road there is a turning to the left leading to the excavations. If you walk up this road, rather than drive further down to the car park and the entrance proper, you will pass on the left the ruins of the vast GYMNASIUM OF VEDIUS and the nearby STADIUM. The gymnasium, built in 150 AD, was once very well appointed with its own baths and latrines. You can see evidence of these today. The stadium is in a very poor state of preservation as much of it has been plundered for building materials.

Further along and to the right of the road you will find the so-called 'Double Church' or CHURCH OF THE VIRGIN MARY (not to be confused with the House of the Virgin Mary). The strange, long and narrow shape of the building is explained by the fact that the church was originally a marketplace.

Continuing down the road, you will reach the car park and an appalling group of souvenir shops, postcard stands and cafes. But fear not; none of this has been allowed to encroach inside the main site itself, which you now enter after paying a small admission fee.

To the right of the tree-lined road are the extensive remains of the HARBOUR GYMNASIUM AND BATHS and directly ahead, the impressive, marble-paved ARCADIAN WAY which leads majestically up from the now dry harbour to the GREAT THEATRE. Underneath the marble paving is an efficient drainage system that runs the length of the street, down to the harbour and connects with the elaborate system that served the whole city. On either side of the street are ruined porticos – galleried walkways, at the back of which shops and shoppers were shaded from the fierce sun. The Arcadian Way even had street lighting, one of the first cities in the world to enjoy such a luxury.

The theatre is huge. It could seat 25,000 people and was used for theatrical entertainments and for festivals dedicated to

Library of Celsus at Ephesus

Artemis. It is still used today for performances during the Ephesus Festival. Climb to the top. It's a long way, but the view is good and it will give you an idea of just how enormous this archaeological site is.

Leaving the theatre, turn left up the MARBLE WAY and follow the road until you reach the magnificently restored LIBRARY OF CELSUS. You can't miss it; the façade is incredibly elaborate. The library was built by a certain Gaius Julius Aquila in 110 AD as a memorial to his father, whose body is still buried in a marble sarcophagus in the burial chamber at the back. The AGORA, currently being excavated is just to the right as you face the library.

·The Marble Way now turns to the left and becomes the STREET OF THE CURETES. The Curetes were an order of priests who served the Goddess Artemis. This was the main street of the town and the most sought after RESIDENTIAL QUARTER. Excavations still continue; to the right of the street can be seen the remains of some of the exclusive houses belonging to wealthy Ephesian citizens and more are currently being restored, further up on the slopes of the hill. Immediately on the left of the street, and facing the library, are the ruins of the city's BROTHEL, identified as such when a number of erotic statues were found during excavations of the site. The next building, fronting the street is the TEMPLE OF HADRIAN. It is a small temple, as temples go, but it has an impressive and beautifully decorated façade. Behind the temple are the BATHS OF SCHOLASTICIA. Scholasticia was a Christian woman who paid for extensive restorations to the baths in the fourth century. Included in the complex are the remains of some very grand public LATRINES.

Heading on up the Street of the Curetes you will find, again on the left, the remains of the FOUNTAIN OF TRAJAN, another Roman emperor. The building once boasted a huge statue of Trajan, but now only the base remains, with one Imperial foot resting possessively on a globe of the world. The street continues past a confusion of ruins awaiting restoration. A little way along, the road forks. Take the right-hand track for a look at the colossal foundations of the TEMPLE OF DOMITIAN before returning back to the main street for a look at the PRYTANEION. This building served both as a town hall and as a temple to Hestia, the goddess of hearth and home. Within the inner sanctuary of the building, burned an eternal flame. Adjoining the Prytaneion is the small ODEON. Much like a miniature theatre, it was used for council meetings, concerts and poetry readings.

You can leave the site at this point and take a taxi or a *dolmuş* either into SELÇUK for a look around the EPHESUS MUSEUM and to see the BASILICA OF ST JOHN, the ISA BEY CAMII and the site of the TEMPLE OF ARTEMIS, or to *Panaghia Kapulu* – the site of the HOUSE OF THE VIRGIN MARY. Alternatively, if you have the energy, you can walk up the path that leads to the GROTTO OF THE SEVEN SLEEPERS.

In the third century, Ephesus was still a pagan city, but there was a growing Christian community. When the reigning emperor paid a visit, he ordered festivities to be held in honour of Artemis and Apollo. Seven young Christians, hoping to escape the mandatory ceremonies, hid themselves in these caves. When they awoke they walked into town to discover that they had slept for 200 years, and that Christianity was now the official State religion. When they died, they were buried in the caves, on the orders of the Christian emperor, and a church was built over them. It has been a holy place, both for Christians and Moslems, for centuries.

It is a widely held belief that *Panaghia Kapulu* was the home of the Virgin Mary. Certainly, Jesus entrusted the care of his mother to John, who is known to have lived in the Ephesus area. In the fourth century a church was built over the site and, although local folklore held that this was Mary's final home, the world at large seemed to have forgotten the place. Little attention was paid until the nineteenth century, when a blind German nun, Catherine Emmerich, who had never set foot outside Germany, claimed that she had seen the Virgin Mary and her final resting place in recurrent dreams. She described in some detail the house where the Virgin Mary had lived, and the tomb in which she was buried. From her descriptions, the house was identified although the tomb has never been discovered. Pope Paul VI visited the site in 1967 and thereby added considerable weight to the story, and the site is now visited by thousands of pilgrims. In Turkish, it is known as *Meryemana* and the Virgin Mary is honoured by Islam as the mother of a great prophet. *Panaghia Kapulu* lies some 5 km from Ephesus. It is a beautiful, peaceful spot and the 'house' has been tastefully restored in a touching and simple fashion.

After you have finished touring the sights of Ephesus, and taken in the Grotto of the Seven Sleepers and *Panaghia Kapulu*, head into the nearby town of Selçuk. This is the settlement to which the remaining inhabitants of Ephesus moved in the sixth century, after the harbour finally became unusable. The town was originally named Ayasoluk, and was chosen as the site of a great church dedicated to St John, and built by the Christian Byzantine Emperor, Justinian. The ruins of this church can be found on the top of the hill that dominates the town. At the foot of the hill is the Isa Bey Camii, built in the early-fourteenth century: What remains is a fine example of Seljuk architecture.

The biggest disappointment in the tour of Ephesus and its surroundings will probably be the remains of the Temple of Artemis. Just a little south-west of the Isa Bey Camii, on the Selçuk-Kuşadasi road, all that remains of this, once, one of the Seven Wonders of the Ancient World, is a rather forlorn column. It stands, often in a pool of water, surrounded by scattered masonry.

Try and find the time to visit the EPHESUS MUSEUM. It contains many finds from the site and will help to bring your visit alive. Unfortunately the museum authorities seem to have a problem with lighting and on occasion many of the priceless artefacts can be plunged into gloom.

KUŞADASI

Your attitude to KUŞADASI will depend very much on what you expect from a holiday resort; and it is very much a holiday resort. It offers plenty of excellent RESTAURANTS, good HOTELS and SHOPS, shops and more shops.

Kuşadasi was included in the itineraries of ships cruising the Aegean, well before the Turkish tourist boom started in earnest. On arrival, passengers were whisked off for a brief tour of the nearby ruined ancient city of Ephesus, and then let loose in the town to shop and eat. They still are. Now as many as eight ships a day visit the town in high season. If you plan to shop, wait for the ships to leave. Prices adjust to a more sensible level.

But what of 'genuine Turkish flavour'? In the centre of the town is a magnificent seventeenth-century CARAVANSERAI. This is now a fancy hotel, with prices to match. The alterations have, fortunately, been carried out sympathetically. Nobody will mind if you wander in through the small door at the front to have a look around.

At the end of a short causeway on the far side of the bay is a small island which offers a well restored GENOESE CASTLE, once the stronghold of the notorious pirate and slaver, Barbarossa. There are excellent views, attractive gardens, a CAFE, RESTAURANT and DISCOTHEQUE.

There are fine BEACHES, ideal for children, on the outskirts of the town. The town beach itself is rather too close to the busy port for clean comfort. If you are looking for lively nightlife the resort offers both 'traditional Turkish evenings' and disco-theques. The Turks are inordinately fond of the latter.

Whatever you may think of Kuşadasi itself, the bay is

attractive and a meal or a drink in one of the quayside restaurants or cafes, watching the sun go down after a heavy day's sightseeing, is a pleasant experience. And this is where Kuşadasi really scores; it is extremely well situated as a base for exploring some of the best Classical sites in Turkey. Ephesus and Selçuk are 15 minutes drive away. Miletus, Priene and Didyma can all be seen in the space of one day, and the sites of Aphrodisias and Bergama (ancient Pergamum) are within reasonable striking distance. A visit to the famous petrified white waterfalls of Pamukkale, together with a detour to Aphrodisias, is possible, though it would be best to stay the night.

PRIENE, MILETUS AND DIDYMA

South of Kuşadasi are the major sites of two ancient RUINED CITIES, and the staggering remains of a TEMPLE OF APOLLO. The three sites can be seen in one day, either by car, or by joining a coach tour from Kuşadasi. You could also go by public transport, a lot more complicated but a great deal more fun. You can take a *dolmuş* to the village of SÖKE, where you have to catch another, bound for GÜLLÜBAHÇE, a village near the ruins of PRIENE. From Priene, take a *dolmuş* bound for AKKÖY and ask to be put off at MILETUS. The driver will almost certainly know where you are going anyway. When you've finished at Miletus, flag down another *dolmuş* bound for Akköy, which will take you south towards DIDYMA.

Priene Perched high on a rock, PRIENE is separated from the sea by 16 km of flat, alluvial plain. It was not always so. Priene, and its neighbour Miletus, were both victims of the silt carried down by the River Menderes, gradually clogging their harbours and strangling their commercial lifeline.

Priene was neither very large, nor very important as a city, and the silting of its harbour made it of even less interest to the Romans, who left it pretty much alone during their occupation of the surrounding area. In most ruined Hellenistic cities, the original buildings stand cheek by jowl with later, Roman edifices. But in Priene, the ruins are pure Greek.

The city was built on the steep slopes of a huge outcrop of rock, in a series of terraces. It is a fine example of a grid-planned Hellenistic city. At the lowest level, are the ruins of the GYMNASIUM and STADIUM, with the AGORA occupying the city centre above.

Further up you can see the well-preserved BOULEUTERION, a council chamber, where the day-to-day government of the city was conducted. To the left of the bouleuterion, as you face the summit, is Priene's principal building – the great TEMPLE OF

ATHENA. Five columns have been re-erected and give a good idea of the original, massive scale.

At the next level up, you will find the small, but very well preserved THEATRE, where you can rest awhile, admire the view, and contemplate scrambling further up the slope to the ruined SANCTUARY OF DEMETER. Above this, the ACROPOLIS looms, some 380 m from the foot of the mountain. You'll probably be glad to know that there is little to see here apart from a stunning view.

Miletus lies 22 km from Priene. It was once the second largest port in the world, with no less than four harbours. It was famed as a cultural centre, and amongst its citizens were numbered eminent historians, geographers and philosophers whose wisdom greatly contributed to the Golden Age of Classical Greece. When the Persians overran Anatolia, Miletus was one of the few cities to attempt a revolt. Gathering support from the other eleven cities who made up the Ionian League, the Miletans attacked the Persian stronghold at Sardis. Disorganised, and generally half-hearted about the venture in the first place, the Ionians were severely defeated and Miletus, as the ringleader of the revolt, was put to the sword. The city was totally destroyed and the few who survived were sold into slavery. When the Persians were eventually defeated by Alexander the Great, the city was rebuilt but never regained its former glory.

Miletus, like its neighbour Priene, eventually fell victim to the silt carried down by the River Menderes, which choked its harbours and deprived the city of its prosperity. There is little left at Miletus today to testify to the glory of this great city, other than a magnificent 15,000 seat GRAECO-ROMAN THEATRE and the remains of the ROMAN BATHS OF FAUSTINA.

Didyma The journey from Miletus to DIDYMA is about 14 km. Didyma was never a city, but the site of a famous oracle and one of the largest and most magnificent temples of the ancient world – the TEMPLE OF APOLLO. The remains are still quite awe-inspiring.

The ancients set great store by oracles, and everyone, from emperors to beggars, came to consult them. They believed that, in certain sacred places, the gods would prophesy the future as well as give general advice, usually through the mediation of a priest or priestess.

At Didyma, a prophetess was installed. Unseen by anyone but the temple priests, she would fast for three days at a time, and breathe the vapours emanating from the sacred spring.

Head of Medusa at Didyma

This seemed to put her into a state of divine inspiration, whereupon she passed obscure messages to the priests, who, acting as middle men, translated them, often into equally obscure verse, for the hopeful clients.

The oracle was active as early as 600 BC, but the Persians destroyed it when they invaded Miletus. It remained inoperative until the arrival of Alexander the Great, when its sacred spring flowed again and the oracle was in business once more. The oracle correctly predicted that one of Alexander's generals, Seleucus, would become a king, and, after Alexander's death, Seleucus set about adding to, and embellishing the temple in a lavish manner. Over the years it suffered from repeated raids and attacks and the building was never completely finished. Nonetheless, it continued to function right up until the Byzantines adopted Christianity as the State religion, and Emperor Theodosius declared that 'no mortal man shall have the effrontery to encourage vain hopes by the inspection of entrails, or attempt to learn the future by the detestable consultation of oracles. The severest penalties await those who disobey.' And so, the fun ended.

Altinkum If you are touring the area, rather than based at Izmir or Kuşadasi, you might feel exhausted enough after tramping round Priene, Miletus and Didyma to opt to stay overnight at the small beach resort of ALTINKUM. Here there is a reasonable selection of HOTELS, RESTAURANTS and PANSIYONS. Altinkum is only 4 km from Didyma.

Bodrum

BODRUM is quite unlike anywhere else in Turkey and it must be said, at the risk of infuriating the Turks, that it looks rather like a prosperous Greek town, with its white, sugar-cube houses, festooned with vivid clumps of flowers. It is one of the few Turkish towns which seems to have developed with some kind of planning in mind.

The focal point of the town is a delightful fourteenth-century CASTLE, perched on a promontory, dividing the two bays around which the town is set.

Long before it became popular with tourists, Bodrum was a haunt of the artistic fraternity, many of them dissident writers and artists who were exiled here. It has a distinctly 'laid-back' and hedonistic atmosphere, and you get the feeling, unlike anywhere else in Turkey, that 'anything goes'. This reputation attracts more and more visitors every year. It's a major yachting centre and the harbour is stiff with every type of boat imaginable, including the beautiful wooden boats built here in Bodrum.

There is no shortage of shops, many of them quite sophisticated by Turkish standards. You can buy leather and jewellery, both of the cheap and cheerful variety and of the type that will put a nasty dent in your holiday budget. You can have sandals custom made, blow your baggage allowance with goodies made of copper and brass, or let yourself get talked into buying a Turkish carpet. The problem with all these shops crowding the town, is that the centre is beginning to resemble a kind of 'Carnaby Street-on-Sea.'

You won't go hungry in Bodrum. Aside from some excellent RESTAURANTS, particularly those overlooking the sea, serving Turkish food, there are plenty of cheaper alternatives – hot savoury and sweet snacks to buy and guzzle in the street, Turkified versions of pizza and hamburger joints and, away from the popular centre of town, cheap working men's *lokantas*.

Entertainment is generally of the noisy variety. Almost every cafe plays Western music, although this is not just common to Bodrum. There are PIANO, JAZZ and WINE BARS and a choice of DISCOTHEQUES.

Bodrum, as you will probably have gathered by now, is not exactly a peaceful spot. If you want a little tranquillity, plan to stay outside Bodrum itself, and use the cheap *dolmuş* network to buzz in and out of town when the fancy takes you.

There are no beaches in Bodrum itself, but boats leave regularly from the harbour to ferry people to less accessible

BEACHES dotted round the peninsula, and there are plenty of small, fishing villages in the area, with good beaches. GÜMBET is the nearest, about 3 km away. This is a suburb of Bodrum and is growing rapidly as more and more hotels and *pansiyons* are built at a furious rate, to cope with the Bodrum overflow. There are RESTAURANTS, CAFES and CAMPSITES, and a long stretch of pebble and shingle BEACH. As the nearest, it is also the most popular, and in high season or on public holidays it gets very full. Alternatives are ORTAKENT (13 km), GÜMÜŞLÜK (25 km) and TURGUT REIS (20 km). The countryside *en route* is so delightful that it makes these beach-hunting trips worthwhile in themselves.

For the cheapest transport, go to the bus station in Bodrum, find a mini-bus or jeep, with your chosen destination written on a card displayed on the windscreen. Get on and wait for it to fill up. When the driver is convinced he can't pack anyone else inside, and you will be convinced before he is, your *dolmuş* will leave. Don't imagine that you will be stranded all day with no food and drink; all of the destinations have at least one RESTAURANT; *dolmuşes* arriving from Bodrum will bounce you back when you've had enough.

The ancient name of Bodrum was Halicarnassus and its most famous citizen was Herodotus – 'the father of history', born in the town in 485 BC. The golden age of Halicarnassus was the fourth century BC, when the ruling king of the region, Mausolus of Caria, made the town his capital. When he died, his wife-sister, Artemisia, succeeded him, and found her own niche in history by building a memorial to her husband, so vast and elaborate, that it was declared one of the Seven Wonders of the Ancient World. Nothing remains of the structure itself, but the original site of the MAUSOLEUM can be found on the outskirts of the town. Earlier finds from the site, excavated in the nineteenth century, are now lodged, along with many other Turkish finds, in the British Museum.

Artemisia, no shrinking violet, is also memorable for having struck a notable blow against male chauvinism. The people of Rhodes, assuming that a woman on the throne would be a push-over, set sail for Halicarnassus with plans to conquer the region. Artemisia hid her fleet in a channel which used to exist behind the castle. When the invaders, finding no opposition, had passed through the mouth of the bay, her ships sallied forth and surrounded the enemy. Heaping indignity upon indignity, she sailed the captured fleet back to Rhodes where the population, turning out in force to greet their victorious navy, were well and truly thrashed.

Bodrum

The CASTLE OF ST PETER was built around 1405 by the Knights of the Order of St John, a multi-racial group of Soldiers of the Cross, who conquered from their base in Rhodes and built the castle to consolidate their foothold on the mainland. It is one of the finest examples of this type of medieval architecture. Now housing Bodrum's MUSEUM, and an open-air THEATRE, it is also the base for the Turkish Underwater Archaeological Institute, and in its numerous halls are displayed the finds from literally hundreds of wrecks sunk off this coast.

In comparison with many of Turkey's museums (even showpiece museums in Istanbul) Bodrum Castle is a gem. The finds are, generally, imaginatively displayed and well-lit. This is particularly true of the glass room where pieces, some dating back as far as the fifteenth century BC, are displayed most effectively in a darkened room.

There are dishes and utensils from the early Bronze Age; jewellery, weapons and bronzes dating back to 1200 BC; all manner of statues and hundreds of amphorae. In the coin section, small plastic models of a loaf of bread, or a house or cow are laid alongside a pile of coins, demonstrating very graphically the value of that particular coinage

The finds are extensive, but a recent survey of the coastline has shown that there are still at least 100 more important wrecks waiting to be excavated. Bodrum sponge-fishermen are given regular lectures by the archaeologists in the castle, telling them precisely what to look out for.

The castle has four towers; head for the 'French' tower first for fine views of Bodrum and the bay. Here you will find the sub-Mycenaean Archaic Age Hall. Now to the 'Italian' tower where you will find the Hellenistic and Classical Hall. After this make a detour to the 'English' tower 'hosted' by a Turkish man and woman dressed respectively as a Knight of St John and a medieval damsel. Here they serve 'flagons' of wine, regardless of the hour, to the accompaniment of jolly 'medieval' music!

The 'German' tower has yet to be opened, but with the 100 or more wrecks off the coastline still to be excavated, it will not be long before the Turks find enough to fill it. The Serpent's Tower houses a collection of ancient amphorae. Still left to see on the way out is the Medieval Hall, the Hall of Coins and Jewellery, the Byzantine Hall and the Bronze Age Hall. The lower courtyard is beautifully landscaped with shady trees and colourful flowers. White doves and magnificent peacocks vie for attention and there is a little CAFE where you can rest awhile.

You can spend a happy few hours wandering alone around the castle, but if you want to be shown round, ask one of the officials at the entrance. If you are lucky, one of the archaeologists, based at the castle, will give you a fascinating conducted tour. There is no charge, but it is considered good form to put some money in the box in the lower courtyard where the tour finishes, and next to where the grain for feeding the doves and peacocks is kept.

Datça If, having explored the castle, seen the site of the mausoleum and the remains of the ancient theatre in Bodrum you want to do more than just laze on the nearby beaches, you could take the ferry to DATÇA, at the tip of the peninsula. If you plan to do this, it would be best to stay there overnight.

Datça is a pleasant alternative for those who might find Bodrum's lively atmosphere a touch too frenetic, and it's a good base for visiting the ruined city of CNIDUS.

Datça is essentially a fishing village, but it is growing in popularity as a resort town and was discovered by the yachting fraternity some time ago. There are HOTELS, PANSIYONS, RESTAURANTS, an unremarkable selection of tourist SHOPS and a reasonable sweep of BEACH, hemming in the village itself. The countryside surrounding Datça is very beautiful.

CNIDUS

You can reach CNIDUS by boat from Bodrum or Marmaris – regular excursion boats are available in season. From Datça there are *dolmuş* boats, again in season, or you can take a taxi. The latter course should not be lightly taken; the road is appalling.

By far the nicest way to see Cnidus is to hitch a ride with a local fisherman. To do this, you will have to be based in Datça the night before and ask around in the bars and restaurants for someone willing to take you. You will then have to get up at a monstrously unsocial hour; but to be at Cnidus, alone at sunrise, is a memorable experience.

Once a thriving harbour city, Cnidus was founded around 700 BC. In 546 BC the populace took up their shovels, with the over-ambitious intention of separating their peninsula from the mainland. They planned to dig out a deep channel, in a bid to halt the advancing Persian army in its tracks. Meanwhile, other more work-shy citizens consulted the oracle at Delphi, who wisely advised against the plan. The Cnidians downed shovels and surrendered without a fight.

Under Persian rule the city thrived as a trading centre, to such an extent that the harbour was unable to handle the increase in shipping. The city was then re-sited, around 400 BC, at the tip of the peninsula, a position which offered the considerable benefit of two natural harbours.

In 334 BC, Cnidus, along with just about everyone else, fell to Alexander the Great. The city, nonetheless, continued to prosper.

A notable cultural centre, Cnidus boasted an advanced school of medicine and an observatory built by the astronomer and mathematician, Eudoxos. Eudoxos actually succeeded in calculating the circumference of the earth with a considerable degree of accuracy.

The city was best known for its controversial statue of Aphrodite. The famous sculptor, Praxiteles, based on the nearby island of Kos, sculpted two statues of the goddess – one clothed, one naked. The islanders were outraged by the latter and the Cnidians, who knew a good investment when they saw one, nipped in smartly and bought it on the cheap. Their presence of mind was amply rewarded. Ships put into port from all points just to snatch a look at the naked goddess. Legend also has it that an opening was made in the rear of the shrine in which the statue was kept, so that sailors could gaze on the goddess' callipygous rump!

Excavations of the ruins were first begun in 1857 by Sir Charles Newton, following his discovery of the site of the Halicarnassus (Bodrum) Mausoleum. As with the Mausoleum, everything of major interest that he unearthed was smartly despatched to the British Museum, in particular a statue of the Goddess Demeter who, together with Aphrodite, was worshipped by the Cnidians. Further work was undertaken by an American archaeologist in 1967, and the site of the circular shrine which housed the notorious statue was discovered – though nothing but a marble block, which may have formed part of the base, was found.

Over the years, the ruins have been repeatedly plundered, and many of the marbles taken and rendered down to lime-powder. Marble was also taken from here to contribute to the building of the Dolmabahçe Palace in Istanbul. As a consequence, what remains are little more than the foundations of TEMPLES, two THEATRES, the larger in a very poor state of preservation, an ODEON, and what is known as the LION TOMB, although the lion which once surmounted it was also whisked away to the British Museum.

Aphrodisias

If you are touring, or staying in the Aegean region, you may well want to travel a little way inland to see the famous sites of APHRODISIAS and PAMUKKALE. Most of the Aegean resorts will offer conducted coach tours, but if you wish to go it alone you can take a bus from any bus-station bound for DENIZLI where you take a *dolmuş* to Pamukkale. On the way to, or from, Denizli you should stop at NAZILLI, which is *en route*, for a *dolmuş* to GEYRE and the ruins of Aphrodisias. You would be well advised to stay overnight in Pamukkale before returning to the coast.

Aphrodisias does not rank with Ephesus in the completeness of its buildings, or with such places as Pergamum, in the drama and majesty of its setting. But it is an undeniably beautiful site, and it's worth the effort, especially as a longish detour on your way to, or from, Pamukkale.

Spread across a plateau, at the foot of BABA DAĞI, Aphrodisias is known to have been inhabited since the sixth century BC, but its heyday was under the Romans, when it was much favoured by successive emperors, and granted many concessions.

Its favoured status with Rome and its prosperity were due almost entirely to the cult of Aphrodite. One of the most celebrated and popular deities of the ancients, her temple at Aphrodisias was famed throughout the world. She was known as the Goddess of Beauty and Love, the queen of laughter, mistress of pleasure and patroness of courtesans; quite a catalogue of hedonistic attributes.

Aphrodisias was also a centre of philosophy, medicine and art. It was renowned for the excellence of its sculptures and during excavations, many fine statues were found, some of which are now displayed in the small MUSEUM on the site.

Under the Byzantines, Christianity took hold and the temple

was converted for use as a church at the end of the fourth century. Following a savage attack in 1402 by the Mongol invader Tamerlane the city declined.

From the museum, follow the path to the monumental HADRIAN'S GATE and head for the 30,000 seat STADIUM. It is in an excellent state of preservation. The remains of the TEMPLE OF APHRODITE, south of the stadium, are not so well preserved and it is hard to imagine what it must have once looked like, before the Christians adapted it for use as a church, and the vicissitudes of weather and earthquake took their toll. Nonetheless, there are a number of columns still standing. In front of the temple is a small ODEON and the ruins of the BISHOP'S PALACE, built in Byzantine times. To the south, amongst the poplar trees, can be found the city's main AGORA, or marketplace. The BATHS OF HADRIAN, beyond the agora, are extensive but well ruined. Heading eastwards you will find the superb, 10,000 seat THEATRE, together with its own complex of BATHS.

PAMUKKALE

Together with the resort of Ölü Deniz on the Mediterranean coast, PAMUKKALE is the star of the Turkish Tourist Board's promotional literature. The problem with all this hype is that your expectations are raised so high, that when confronted with the real thing, you're invariably disappointed. Having said that, Pamukkale is an extraordinary sight and you will never see anything quite like it anywhere else.

Tour companies run excursions here from Kuşadasi, Izmir, Bodrum and Marmaris. Most will include a visit to Aphrodisias on the way and put you up overnight in one of the motels at Pamukkale. If you go independently, take a bus to DENIZLI and then a *dolmuş* for the short trip to Pamukkale. Unless you have booked ahead, you probably won't get a bed in one of the fancier hotels, especially in season. But in the village below Pamukkale, there is a selection of *pansiyons* and inexpensive hotels which vary from incredibly basic to folksy-but-comfortable.

'Pamukkale' means 'cotton castle', not a bad description of the place. Water gushing from the natural hot thermal springs of nearby Hierapolis is so rich in limestone that, over the centuries, deposits have built up on the ridges of the cliff face and formed themselves into fantastical, snow-white petrified waterfalls. At the upper levels an unceasing flow of water has carved out a series of terraces that constantly fill and spill over with warm spring water.

'Cotton castle' at Pamukkale

You can paddle about in this centrally heated fairyland, climbing from rock pool to rock pool, or swim in one of the pools belonging to the modern HOTELS strung out along the ridge. These pools are fed by the same, hot spring waters.

The approach road to Pamukkale takes you up, past the turning on the left for the small, but rapidly expanding village at the foot of the cliff, to the plateau at the top. Unfortunately the authorities have allowed a shanty town of souvenir shops to spread along the side of the road, and their tawdriness sits ill with the natural wonder of Pamukkale.

Hierapolis When you've had enough of the 'cotton castle', take a leisurely stroll and have a look at the ruins of the site of ANCIENT HIERAPOLIS. The best-preserved ruins are not far away although the site is quite extensive and you would need a whole day to see everything on foot.

The same hot spring waters that flow down to Pamukkale today, fed the ancient city. Hierapolis means 'Sacred City', a name earned as a result of the supposed healing properties of the water. The city was founded in 190 BC by Eumenes II, King of Pergamum, whose successor Attalus III willed all his kingdom to the Romans on his death. Under Roman rule the city was extensively developed, and despite the frequent earthquakes, it flourished as a popular spa centre. During the Byzantine era the city was a stronghold of Christianity and a large church was built here, dedicated to the Apostle Philip who had lived in Hierapolis and was martyred in AD 80.

Yet another earthquake destroyed the city in AD 1334 and this time the populace gave up and abandoned it.

Near the souvenir shops you will find the original ROMAN BATHS. A private section was reserved for visiting emperors. One of the halls in the baths complex houses a small MUSEUM, displaying finds discovered during excavations of the area. Near the baths you will find the remains of a TEMPLE OF APOLLO and the grotto, or SANCTUARY OF PLUTO, known in ancient times as the Plutonium. Together with the healing powers of the waters, it is the Plutonium that was chiefly responsible for the fame of Hierapolis. Pluto, God of the Underworld, apparently manifested himself by means of toxic gases escaping into the atmosphere from a fissure in the rock. Ancient historians tell us that ordinary mortals perished if they inhaled the fumes. Priests however, especially eunuch priests, appeared to be immune, which must have done a great deal to increase their power and influence over the congregation. The Turks now call this spot the *Cin Deliği*, the 'Devil's Hole'. Further on is the 15,000 seat THEATRE and in spite of the fact that one section has collapsed it is still very impressive.

Hierapolis has a truly enormous NECROPOLIS, when you consider that its main claim to fame was as a health spa. Spread to the north and south of the site, outside the ruined city walls, are hundreds and hundreds of tombs. If you have the time, head northwards where there is the greatest concentration of sarcophagi. Even if tomb-spotting doesn't grab your imagination, it's a lovely area for walking.

C·H·A·P·T·E·R· 6

The Mediterranean Coast

Marmaris

It's hard to describe the MARMARIS region without sounding like an over-written holiday brochure but it is a beautiful spot, and while the town itself is unremarkable, its setting is a dream.

Looking out across the sea from the main promenade, you could be forgiven for imagining you were in Norway. Marmaris itself is situated on a huge, virtually land-locked, fjord-like bay, closely flanked by thickly forested mountains. The surrounding shores are peppered with tiny, isolated coves and beaches.

Once the ancient port of Physkus, Marmaris prospered as a stopping off point on the busy Anatolian-Rhodes-Egypt trade route, and it was a strategic base for Süleyman the Magnificent's assault on Rhodes in 1522. The only historical site of note in the town is the CASTLE, dating from this period, built

Typical Turkish yacht

on a hill behind the yacht harbour. Once you've clambered up to the battlements for a good view of the town and the bay, you can indulge yourself on the beaches and in the relatively sophisticated fleshpots of Marmaris with a clear conscience, as, apart from excursions, you've seen the lot.

Marmaris is a major yachting centre and virtually every type of pleasure craft, from opulent gin-palaces to small, brightly-coloured Turkish *Kayıks* line the yacht harbour and part of the promenade.

There are plenty of BEACHES accessible by road, but some of the nicest are best visited by boat. Stroll along the palm-tree lined promenade in the early evening and you will see numerous craft displaying details of the trips for the following day. Here too you can take a day trip to Rhodes, about 2½ hours by ferry. Tour companies all over the town can make the necessary arrangements for you. (You may have to give up your passport the night before the trip, so make arrangements the day before you plan to go.)

Many of the big hotels are outside Marmaris itself and in high season this is the place to be as the town can get very crowded and, in common with most popular holiday resorts, extremely noisy. The *dolmuş* system makes it easy and cheap to pop in and out of town when you want the high life. Go in the early evening and bag yourself a front row seat in one of the many

BARS and CAFES that line the front; here you can watch the best free show in Marmaris – the changing colours over the bay as the sun sets.

The main concentration of restaurants is along the promenade and many of these are excellent. Venture further into the town itself and prices will generally be lower; the further you move away from the tourist attractions at the sea-front the cheaper prices will be.

FETHIYE

The town that once occupied the site of FETHIYE was the ancient Lycian city, Telmessus. Today nothing remains of the settlement but a collection of extraordinary Lycian ROCK TOMBS; examples can be seen carved into the mountainside behind the town.

Lycian rock-cut tombs

The Lycians went to a great deal of trouble to bury their dead, carving intricately façaded burial-chambers out of solid rock. The tombs were designed to look like either temples, or houses, reflecting the style of the wooden houses in which the Lycians actually lived. A fine example of the temple-style tomb can be seen here – The TOMB OF AMYNTAS, dating from around 400 BC. In the town itself are a number of Lycian STONE TOMBS (sarcophagi). You can see a particularly good example, with fine carvings depicting scenes of city life, near the Post Office, and as you wander round the town you will stumble on others, in all sorts of unlikely places.

Aside from all this funerary paraphernalia there are the ruins of a MEDIEVAL CASTLE, atop a hill overlooking the town. The castle is believed to have been built by the Knights of St John on top of the remains of an ancient site dating back to 400 BC.

Fethiye itself is not particularly prepossessing. A serious earthquake destroyed much of the town in 1958, and the replacement buildings are uninspiring. But the setting is lovely, on a broad bay, dotted with small islands, furrowed by inlets and coves with pine forests to the water's edge. In common with Marmaris and Bodrum, its well protected harbour makes it popular with yachtsmen. There are CAFES, RESTAURANTS and SHOPS at intervals along the waterfront, but the best that the town has to offer can be found in the network of narrow streets in the centre, a little north of the main waterfront street. Here, amongst the ubiquitous carpet shops, are some delightful restaurants. The atmosphere at night is lively, and the food often excellent. Sometimes groups of Turkish musicians can be found strolling from restaurant to restaurant and table to table delighting (or, depending on your mood, annoying) you with jolly Turkish ditties.

Fethiye offers DISCOTHEQUES and NIGHTCLUBS to keep you active well into the night and if, the following morning, you need something more than a swim to get yourself going again, try the attractive TURKISH BATH which you will find in the centre of town a little way inland from the main waterfront street. They are well used to tourists.

There is no beach in Fethiye itself, but boats can be taken from the town seafront every day, to visit the clusters of islands and the good beaches further round the bay. *Dolmuşes* provide a cheap ferrying service for those beaches accessible by road.

ÖLÜ DENIZ

The resort of ÖLÜ DENIZ, easily reached by *dolmuş*, is 15 km from Fethiye. It is one of the brightest jewels in Turkey's tourist crown, and it is heavily promoted as a BEACH PARADISE. Ölü Deniz literally means 'Dead Sea' and its name derives from a sheltered lagoon, bordered by a huge sweep of fine shingle beach, with only a small inlet from the sea, denying access to large boats. The water is exceptionally warm and calm; wonderful for young children.

Ölü Deniz hasn't suffered yet from the kind of concrete jungle development usually inevitable in this kind of beauty spot, but there are HOTELS and a number of rather untidy CAMPSITES which the photographs you will see of the place manage to keep well out of frame.

You have to pay to use the lagoon beach itself (only a nominal amount) but there are plenty of other beaches strung out around the bay which offer excellent bathing. As you arrive at the resort, immediately in front of you, there is a long stretch of beach lined with a shanty town of RESTAURANTS and CAFES, almost all of them playing loud Western pop music. To the right is the road that takes you to the lagoon itself, but if peace and quiet is what you want follow the track to the left. The further you venture, the better will be your reward. In mid and high season *dolmuşes* ply the route.

Ölü Deniz offers a selection of EATERIES and DISCO-THEQUES; if you want good Turkish food, go into Fethiye. Ölü Deniz may be a beach paradise, but a gourmet's paradise it is not.

Fethiye and Ölü Deniz both make a good base for exploring the historic and archaeological sites that litter the region. To do them justice you really need a car, but there are organised tours to some of the larger sites and, if there are enough of you, it is often possible to negotiate for a private taxi to some of the nearer spots, without breaking the budget.

If you are making for Antalya and the eastern Mediterranean you can take the route inland over the mountains. Up until quite recently this was a fairly hair-raising experience, but the road has been considerably improved and the countryside is magnificent.

The other choice is the coastal route and it is from this road that the majority of the ancient sites, with the exception of Tlos, can be reached.

Tlos

TLOS was one of the oldest and most powerful cities in the Lycian Federation. It remained an important city through the Byzantine period and was still inhabited in the nineteenth century, when the pirate Kanli Ali Ağa used part of the Ottoman Castle as his winter quarters.

About an hour's drive from Fethiye, Tlos is reached by turning right off the Fethiye-Korkuteli road at the small town of KEMER. The site is worth a visit if only for its magnificent setting, high on a rocky promontory with the Taurus mountains to the east and the plain of Xanthos to the west.

The ruins themselves have never been excavated and are fast disappearing under a spreading carpet of vegetation. The effect is wild and romantic. To do the site justice you should be prepared for something of a scramble. At the foot of the site is the small village of KALEASAR, where the children, part amateur historians, part mountain goats, will happily act as your guides.

The remains of a TURKISH FORTRESS dominate the site; from here the view of the plains and mountains quite takes your breath away. Look too at the ROMAN THEATRE, still impressive in its choking mantle of weeds, the remains of the STADIUM and the BATHS, and at the ROCK TOMBS, the most interesting of which is a temple tomb with three doors. The centre door is purely ornamental, whilst the other two give access to the funeral chamber. On the façade of the tomb is a relief of Bellerophon astride Pegasus, poised to kill the fire-breathing Chimaera; the original rulers of Tlos believed they were descended from Bellepheron.

The legend of Bellerophon Bellerophon was the son of King Glaucus of Corinth. In expiation of a murder, Bellerophon exiled himself to the court of King Proteus. Here, the king's wife promptly fell in love with him and when her efforts to seduce him were spurned, she told her husband that Bellerophon had raped her. Unable to bring himself to execute the handsome young man, the king despatched him to the court of Iobates, his father-in-law, with a sealed message asking Iobates to do his dirty work for him. Iobates decided to set Bellerophon a series of impossible tasks, during the course of which he was bound to perish. The first of these was to kill the Chimaera, a disagreeable fire-breathing monster with the head of a lion, the body of a goat and the tail of a serpent, who lived in the mountains of Lycia.

Bellerophon was given a set of golden reins by the Goddess Athena with which he was able to control the winged horse, Pegasus. Astride Pegasus, Bellerophon launched a surprise aerial attack and stuffed a spear heavily tipped with lead into the monster's gaping jaws. In the heat of the Chimaera's breath the lead melted and the monster choked to death.

Returning unscathed from a further series of dangerous

tasks, Bellerophon, his innocence now proved, married the king's daughter and became heir to Lycia.

PINARA

Ancient PINARA was another important city in the Lycian Federation, and is known to have existed as far back as the fifth century BC. The site has long been abandoned by the excavators and the extensive ruins are overgrown, but for the enthusiast, it's well worth a visit.

The most dramatic sight is a huge outcrop of rock with a rounded peak, the east face of which is honeycombed with hundreds of tombs. Not the elaborate carved house and temple tombs, but simple, rectangular openings, The mind boggles imagining how these must have been carved and how the bodies must have been lowered for burial inside.

To reach the Pinara site, you must turn right, off the main Fethiye to Kaş road. Follow the signposted track to the village of MINARE where you must abandon the car – you will be glad to by then, for the road is not good – and scramble up to the site. If you just want to take a look at the 'Honeycomb Mountain' from a comfortable distance, drive on through the village and a short while after the road curves round to the right, the rock can be seen behind you.

LETOON

THE LETOON was the sacred city of Lycia; Leto was Lycia's national deity – hence the name.

Legend has it that Leto, pregnant by Zeus, was on the run from the jealous fury of Zeus' wife Hera. On the island of Delos, Leto gave birth to Apollo and Artemis; but when Hera discovered her hiding-place, Leto was forced to gather up her children and flee to Lycia. Stopping to quench her thirst and bathe her children in a spring, she was chased away by shepherds. They paid dearly for their disagreeable behaviour, for Leto promptly turned them into frogs.

She was finally guided to the banks of the Xanthos river by wolves. In recognition of their service, she renamed the land, hitherto known as Termilis – Lykos or Lycia, 'for the wolves'.

Much of the ruins of the Letoon are submerged but it is worth a visit for the beauty of its setting and for the wildlife. Go in the evening and you will hear the descendants of the frog-shepherds croaking their indignation.

The foundations of three ancient TEMPLES can still be seen; one dedicated to Leto, and one to Apollo and Artemis. The smaller, central temple is as yet unidentified.

The ruins of a BYZANTINE CHURCH, destroyed in the seventh century during the Arab invasions, and a huge, half-submerged NYMPHAEUM can be seen just beyond the temples. On the hillside to the north you can find Letoon's Hellenistic THEATRE with two tunnel passages.

The Letoon can be reached by turning right, off the main Fethiye-Kaş-Antalya road. The ancient site will be reached after about 4 km.

Xanthos

Few are enthusiastic enough to want to stop at every Classical ruin on the coastal route from Fethiye to Antalya. Those who would like to see an accessible selection, would do well to stop at XANTHOS. The ruins are just off the main road, and have the advantage of sparing you and your car the bone-shattering ride over stony tracks, unavoidable with most of the other sites. You will find Xanthos about 50 km along the Fethiye-Kaş-Antalya road to the left, just as you come into the unprepossessing, little town of KINIK.

Nereids' Tomb

128

Xanthos was the capital city of the Lycian Federation and a force to be reckoned with as far back as 1200 BC. Homer mentions its involvement in the Trojan War, but we have no real information about Xanthos until 545 BC when the powerful Persian army turned up at the gates. Resistance against such an overwhelming force was futile. But resist the citizens did, with tragic results. Penned up in their city they moved their women and children to the highest point and burned the city to the ground. Swearing to each other that they would fight to the death, the men left the relative safety of the besieged acropolis to face the might of the Persian army. They perished to a man.

Herodotus tells us that 80 Xanthian families were away from the city at the time. It was they who returned and founded the new Xanthos. The Xanthians were sensibly less hot-headed when faced with Alexander the Great in 333 BC; they submitted to his demands, gaining in exchange a considerable degree of freedom.

In 42 BC, caught in the crossfire of the Roman civil wars, the city was to suffer another major blow. Brutus, desperate for money and troops to fight Mark Antony and Octavian, arrived to extort taxes from the Lycians. The Xanthians chose to resist. Once again they were besieged in their city and faced with overwhelming odds. Again they set fire to the city, throwing their wives and children into the flames, and set about committing mass suicide. Brutus, moved to tears by their cries, offered a bonus to his soldiers for every Xanthian saved. The soldiers moved in to put an end to the self-inflicted carnage but only 150 Xanthians survived.

Against all the odds, Xanthos bounced back. With aid from the Romans much of the city was rebuilt and Xanthos, once again, became the most important city in Lycia. The final decline of the city coincided with that of the Roman Empire, although Xanthos was still inhabited up to the twelfth century AD.

To get a good idea of Xanthos' former glory, you need look no further than London. In 1838, following a British naval survey of this part of the Mediterranean coastline, Sir Charles Fellows discovered the site, and two years later a contingent of sailors was despatched to excavate the pick of the ruins and ship them back to the British Museum.

On the left as you come up the track from Kinik, are the remains of the TRIUMPHAL ARCH of Vespasian, dating from around 70 AD. A little further up on the right is a parking area; walk back to take a look at the foundations of the TEMPLE-TOMB OF THE NEREIDS. The temple itself was taken, piece by piece, and can now be seen, reconstructed in the British Museum.

To the left of the track heading away from Kinik, you will find the remains of a ROMAN THEATRE, which now stands on part of the site occupied by the twice burned Lycian acropolis. The Orchestra is now a jumble of fallen masonry. Here, too, you can see the famous 'HARPIES' TOMB' dating from the fifth century BC. The tomb was once decorated with fine reliefs all round the upper, funerary chamber. The reliefs can be seen today, but they are only plaster casts. The originals, again, are in the British Museum.

The tomb derives its name from the strange half-woman, half-bird creatures depicted on the friezes, carrying children in their arms. These were believed to be the mythical Harpies, an unpleasant bunch who made a habit of stealing children to give as servants to the Furies. It is now believed that the 'birdwomen' are benign spirits, carrying off the souls of the dead to the Isles of the Blessed.

Next to the Harpies' Tomb there is an unusual LYCIAN PILLAR TOMB. The pillar section is hollow and contains a funeral chamber, whilst the sarcophagus atop the pillar contains another chamber, added at a later date.

A number of other tombs, the vestiges of a ROMAN ACROPOLIS and a BYZANTINE MONASTERY can be explored by taking the path from the parking area.

If you still have an appetite for more in the way of Lycian tombs, you can head northwards, away from the car park towards the old NECROPOLIS. Here you will find tombs aplenty – rock-cut tombs, pillar tombs and sarcophagi, some with elaborate and skilful carvings.

While you are exploring the site, you will probably be hailed by the 'guardian' who languishes under an awning just beyond the theatre. He will sell you a cold drink and a book on Lycian cities, but you are unlikely to get an impromptu guided tour. Nobody who has been there has seen him move!

PATARA

There are two good reasons for suffering the bumpy 15 km detour off the main road to PATARA. If you haven't had enough of ancient Lycian cities there are more than enough ruins here to keep you happily exploring for hours and if you have, you will find, just beyond the site of the ancient harbour city, one of the most impressive BEACHES in Turkey. A vast expanse of golden sand stretches out as far as the eye can see. The walk over the wide beach to the edge of the water is hard going, especially in the heat of the day, as the sand is fine and deep, but if a clean, uncrowded, sandy beach, offering excellent swimming is what you want, then this is the place to go. At the end of the track leading to the beach, there is a small RESTAURANT.

In common with other Lycian cities, Patara had the good sense not to resist Alexander the Great, and after his death adapted itself quietly to a succession of rulers. Unlike the Xanthians, after a token resistance, the Patarans submitted to Brutus' extortionate tax demands and survived to reap the benefits, as a centre from which Rome controlled the region, and the only port in Lycia able to service the Roman fleet. Hadrian had a vast GRANARY built here to store grain awaiting transport to Rome. The building is roofless, but still in a remarkable state of preservation.

Patara was an important centre of Christianity. From here St Paul set sail on his final journey to Rome, and St Nicholas was born here. But Patara's main claim to fame was as the site of the ORACLE OF APOLLO, vying with that of Delphi in the sagacity of its pronouncements. It was nonetheless a little erratic. Apparently the oracle could only function when Apollo was in residence, and since the god favoured Delos for his summer break, the Patara oracle only functioned in the winter months. Neither the Temple of Apollo, nor the oracle, can be seen today. Future excavations may reveal the site, but they will have to battle against the constant encroachment of the sand which is inexorably burying the city.

Patara's prosperity was based on her port facilities, but during the late-fourteenth century the harbour gradually began to silt up. Soon it was impassable for ships of any substantial size and Patara rapidly fell into decline.

What there is to be seen today is scattered to the west of the road. To the south, huge sand dunes block the ruins and the mouth of the old harbour from the seashore. Just in front of the dunes is the THEATRE, well preserved but increasingly obscured by drifting sand.

On the hill above the theatre is a curious circular pit with a pillar in the centre. There is a rock-cut stairway leading to the bottom. There is no consensus as to what this pit was for. Some claim it is the site of the oracle, but most assume it was a cistern and that the pillar once supported a roof.

From the top of the hill you can take stock of your surroundings and decide whether to struggle through the sand and undergrowth to see the rest of Patara. The ROMAN GRAIN STORE is to the west, on the far side of the old harbour. To the east, accessible from the approach road, is the TRIPLE-

ARCHED GATEWAY, the original entrance to the city, still in remarkable condition although the statues which would have graced the empty niches, have long since gone. South of the triple arch you will find the ruins of some BATHS, but venture a little further southwards and you will find, in much better condition, the BATHS OF VESPASIAN. Between the two baths there is a small, well-preserved CORINTHIAN TEMPLE with rich carvings on the door lintel.

In keeping with the Lycian passion for funerary art, the whole area is littered with SARCOPHAGI. Everywhere, livestock, belonging to the local village, graze contentedly amongst the ruins.

The track to Patara can be found to the right, off the main Fethiye-Kaş-Antalya road.

KALKAN

Only a short hop from Kaş, KALKAN is the next resort town along this coastline. If it wasn't for the relatively new yacht marina, Kalkan would probably have remained a sleepy little fishing village. As it is, the flotillas have discovered it, and in season it can be swarming with yachtsmen, especially in the evenings.

Although the magnificent Patara beach is not far away, there are no beaches in the vicinity of Kalkan itself. This alone should stop this picturesque little village from becoming unpleasantly over-developed.

KAŞ

KAŞ developed firstly as a working fishing village, and secondly as a yacht-provisioning centre. It was never planned with tourism in mind and, because of this, it has more of a Turkish atmosphere than almost any of the other seaside resorts along the Aegean or Mediterranean coasts.

The view of Kaş from the approach road, high up in the encircling mountains, is stunning, particularly at sunset. The town straggles out round the shores of a wide bay, thickly forested with mountain pine. Narrow streets with old, red-tiled Turkish houses, their wooden balconies jutting out over the street, radiate from the central focus of the town – the harbour.

There is a good selection of RESTAURANTS and BARS, mostly around the harbour area, and in a covered street leading north from the harbour up to the town's bus-station. There is a wide promenade that follows the curve of the harbour, where you can sit and enjoy ice cream or soft drinks. There is no shortage of shops, especially carpet shops, but nothing particularly sophisticated.

There is no beach in the town itself, except for a tiny cove reached by walking a short distance up the road east from the harbour. It's on the right, just over the brow of the hill, past the barracks. It's a steep climb down. Further out, on both sides of the bay, there are pebble coves and places where you can swim from the rocks. If you want a good sandy beach you should make for Patara (described previously). Tour companies in Kaş organise visits to Patara, but these are often combined with visits to other nearby ruins, so if it's only the beach you're after, it's worth checking to see if a *dolmuş* is going from the bus-station. Make sure that it takes you right down to Patara. If you get jettisoned on the main road, you'll have a dusty, 6 km walk.

Kaş was once the ancient trading harbour town of Antiphellos, but most of the ancient settlement is covered by the modern town. Aside from a small THEATRE on the western edge, there is little else to see, other than more examples of Lycian funerary art, though there are beautiful views across the sea to the tiny Greek island of Kastellorizon which can be clearly seen from Kaş. Day trips are organised in season to Kastellorizon. The trip takes about 40 minutes; no passports are

Lycian sarcophagus

required as the island is not an official port of entry to Greece. On the hill behind the theatre you will find an interesting Lycian ROCK-CUT TOMB dating from the fourth century BC. The inner chamber of the tomb is decorated with a frieze depicting 21 tiny dancing figures. Two Lycian SARCOPHAGI can be found in the town itself, one in the harbour area and one in the square reached by walking up the street on the eastern corner of the harbour square.

Kekova and Simena

You can reach SIMENA by car, turning right, off the Kaş-Antalya road, signposted to Kekova and Kale. But it's more pleasant and practical to see the sites by boat; regular day trips are available from Kaş. If there's enough of you, or your budget allows, you can negotiate for a private boat trip, either from Kaş or from the harbour near Demre further east along the coast.

Many of the ancient sites around this coastline have submerged as a result of earthquakes; the main point of this trip is to see the outlines of the ruined cities beneath the surface of the water. In general that is exactly what they are – just outlines. But they are still a wonderful and fascinating sight as long as you don't let your expectations get too out of hand.

The standard trip from Kaş skirts the underwater ruins of APERLAE: beneath the surface you can see the vestiges of the quay, the outline of streets and the foundations of buildings. Next, the boat makes a stop at KEKOVA ISLAND, in a tiny bay where you can swim in the clear waters and peer at more ruins beneath the surface. At the edge of the stony beach is the ruined apse of a BYZANTINE CHURCH. It is a most attractive spot.

Crossing back to the mainland, the boat heads for the site of ancient Simena stopping for lunch at KALE. Here a cluster of houses straggles up the steep hill, with a few simple RESTAURANTS at the foot. At the top is a fine BYZANTINE FORTRESS. It's a steep climb but worth the effort for the view. On the way up, you will be importuned by peasant women and children lining the path, to buy a selection of local handicrafts, hopeful that breathless tourists will show scant resistance to their sales technique. Near the top, inside the castle walls, is a little THEATRE with seven rows of seats cut entirely out of the rock-face. The theatre seated 300 people.

Demre and Myra

The coastal road from Kaş to Antalya has recently undergone some much needed improvement, and although there are still rough patches, the route is generally good.

As you approach Demre the road drops sharply to the town. You could be forgiven for thinking that you were looking at rice fields in the valley below. But as you arrive, you'll see that these are in fact greenhouses. Hundreds and hundreds of them.

As a town, Demre is ugly and dusty, but it's worth stopping to see the ancient ruined CITY OF MYRA, and while you're there you could take a look at the CHURCH OF ST NICHOLAS (better known to Westerners as Father Christmas).

St Nicholas was born further west, in Patara, but he was Bishop of Myra; this is where he lived and died and where the legend that eventually led to Christmas stockings began. A wealthy man in his own right, St Nicholas used to give anonymous gifts of dowries to the girls of poor families in his diocese.

Follow the yellow signs for *Baba Noel* and you will find the Church of St Nicholas in the town itself. The church and burial chapel were built following his death in 3 AD, but the site has undergone various modifications and repairs since then, and was in fact used as a mosque until quite recently. Then it dawned on the authorities what a unique tourist attraction they had in the midst of their dusty little town.

In 1087 the remains of St Nicholas were stolen and spirited off to Italy where trade in grisly relics was a very lucrative business. The robbers left a few bones behind in their haste to get away, and these can be seen, if the fancy takes you, in the Antalya Museum.

On the left as you enter through the gate is a BRONZE STATUE of St Nicholas depicted as the fat, jolly Santa Claus complete with his sack of presents and his cotton-wool beard. A little further on you descend to the church itself. Inside there are patches of mosaic and the colours of wall paintings are still quite vivid.

If you are short of time you could give the church a miss, but it would be a shame not to see the ancient site of Myra, on the outskirts of the town. The approach to the site takes you through a dusty street lined with ramshackle greenhouses. With an incongruous lack of ceremony you are suddenly faced with ancient Myra. Another example of the juxtaposition of the sublime and the mundane found throughout Turkey.

Ancient Myra was one of the 'Big Six' within the Lycian Federation, and continued to flourish under Roman rule. St Paul stopped here on his way to Rome. In the Byzantine era it was a centre of religious and administrative affairs, and the popularity and renown of its foremost bishop, St Nicholas, helped retain its prominence longer than other Lycian cities. It fell foul, eventually, of the forces of nature. Myra's harbour,

Andriake, gradually silted up. The remains of the ancient city are now over 5 km from the sea.

The first thing you will notice as you approach the site is the steep cliff-face riddled with Lycian ROCK-CUT TOMBS. Many of these can be explored by scrambling up steps cut into the rock-face. You don't have to be a mountaineer, but the higher levels are not for those of a nervous disposition. The site guardian is more than willing to lend a helping hand, and using a *pot-pourri* of languages, he will give you a guided tour. Don't be fooled by him; he may appear long in the tooth, but he's as nimble as a mountain-goat, and he'll expect you to follow doggedly wherever he goes.

There are house-style tombs, temple tombs and simple cell tombs. Once inside, you can tell the size of the family by the number of 'shelves' provided, on which to lay the bodies. The hollow in the centre of some of the tombs is a receptacle for food and drink, to sustain the departed on their journey across the river Styx. The façades of many of the tombs are richly decorated with elaborate reliefs and there are numerous inscriptions. Unfortunately, unless your Lycian is up to scratch, they won't mean a great deal.

The best place to start your exploration is at the base of the cliff where you will find Myra's impressive GRAECO-ROMAN THEATRE. Numerous earthquakes have left their mark, but amidst the chaotic heaps of broken masonry in and around the site of the theatre, you can still find blocks or fragments bearing elaborate friezes, mostly from the partially collapsed stage-building, illustrating just how magnificent the theatre must have been before nature did her worst.

Having explored Myra you could make the short trip to the harbour, ANDRIAKE, once Myra's port, where you can relax on the reasonable BEACH, or arrange for a boat trip to the sunken ruins of Kekova.

Finike Continuing along the Antalya road from Demre, you will pass through the small coastal town of FINIKE. A few small yachts put in here as a quiet stop-off point on the Mediterranean coast, but Finike seems to have missed out on the beautiful setting stakes, and this alone is likely to keep it free from major tourist invasion. There are some RESTAURANTS along the seafront road and it makes an agreeable place for a lunch on your way to or from Antalya.

OLYMPOS

You have to take a 9 km detour off the main road to get to OLYMPOS, and the track is rough. If you go expecting well-preserved ruins, you will be very disappointed. What remains is in poor condition, difficult to identify and mostly submerged under a carpet of vegetation. But, as a beauty spot it's worth the trouble. Surrounded by mountains, the site is bisected by a crystal clear rushing stream. You can potter from bank to bank amongst the pink oleanders by way of stepping stones, or pick your way along the banks to the beautiful pebble BEACH at the mouth of the estuary.

North-west from Olympos, one hour's stiff walking will take you to the perpetual flame that gave rise to the legend of the CHIMAERA – the fire-breathing monster of the underworld slain by Bellerophon astride the winged horse Pegasus. Don't expect a dramatic inferno; it's a feeble display and unless you are blessed with the most fertile of imaginations, generally a disappointment.

PHASELIS

The easternmost city of ancient Lycia, PHASELIS, was originally colonised from Rhodes in the seventh century BC. The city prospered as an important and strategically situated trading port – it has three natural harbours. In 333 BC the Phaselitians fell over themselves to surrender to Alexander the Great, who was so taken with the city's attractive setting, 'the midwinter roses in full bloom, the scent of lilies . . .' that he halted his armies and settled in Phaselis for the winter.

Under the Romans the city prospered, but from the third century AD it was plagued by pirate raids. By the seventh century Phaselis had seriously declined and was no match for the frequent Arab invasions. There was a revival of fortunes under the Byzantine Empire, and money was found to rebuild and strengthen the city and its harbours; but by the twelfth century, under Seljuk sovereignty, Phaselis began to play second fiddle to the nearby trading ports of Antalya and Alanya and the city fell into decline.

To see the site today involves a short detour on a good road from the main Kaş-Antalya highway. Phaselis is only a short distance from Antalya and is consequently a favourite holiday spot for the locals. You have to pay a small admission fee, but although the ruins are not extensive, there is a good shingle BEACH and it is a lovely spot when not too crowded, to laze away the day.

Before you explore the ruins you might find it worthwhile to have a quick look inside the small MUSEUM at the entrance to the site. Here you will see the layout of the city as it was, photographs of different stages of the excavations, and the few artefacts found on the site that haven't been carried off to other, grander, museums.

All of the ruins to be seen here date from the Roman and Byzantine eras. There is a well preserved street, once the city's main thoroughfare, leading from the central, city harbour. To the left of the street, heading towards the south harbour, is a delightful, overgrown THEATRE. Further on you will find the remains of a GATEWAY built in honour of the visit of Hadrian to the city around 130 AD.

KEMER

KEMER is a purpose-built holiday village, and feverish building is still very much in evidence. It has a newly equipped YACHT MARINA and everything else you would expect of a modern resort town. It is quite well located for exploring the spectacular countryside to the west (Phaselis, Olympos, Myra, Kekova) and for heading east to the city of Antalya and the sites of Perge, Aspendos and Side, or inland to Termessos. All of these can be visited in day trips of varying lengths. But, if you want to stay somewhere with a genuine Turkish flavour, you would be well advised to opt for either Kaş or Side.

ANTALYA

A bustling modern city, ANTALYA is one of the largest in Turkey. It sits on the borders of ancient Lycia to the west and ancient Pamphylia to the east, and is a good base from which to explore the ruined cities of both regions.

Antalya was originally called Attaleia, after King Attalus of Pergamum, and it was he who founded the city in the second century BC. Although it already possessed a good natural harbour, it wasn't developed until after Attalus failed to bring the nearby port of Side to heel. Antalya then became a naval base and a stronghold from which Attalus attempted, not very successfully, to control the plain of Pamphylia. Continually plagued by pirates, the city was eventually taken in hand by the Romans and then the Byzantines. In the thirteenth century, from their stronghold in Konya, the Seljuk Turks conquered the city. In 1391 the Ottomans took over. Antalya, unlike the deserted cities dotting the coastline to the east and west, has been continually inhabited and, as a result, most of the ruins of earlier structures are buried under later building works, or have been dismantled for building materials over the years.

The modern town has its fair share of hideous tower blocks and nondescript suburbs, but it is splendidly situated atop the

Fluted Minaret in Antalya

cliffs surrounding a wide crescent bay, with the Taurus mountains providing a dramatic backcloth.

Of all the sights to see in Antalya, the YIVLI MINARE, or Fluted Minaret is the easiest to locate. This pinkish minaret towers above the city, and is one of the few Seljuk buildings still intact. The six-domed building at the base of the minaret was originally a Byzantine church, then a mosque and finally a museum.

From here you can easily walk to all the sites worth seeing in the city. Take one of the narrow winding streets down the hill through the old town of Antalya. The authorities have, fortunately, seen fit to slap a preservation order on this part of the town, and the charming old Turkish houses give a good idea of what an Ottoman town must have looked like.

From here you can climb the steep steps to the top of the cliff that overlooks the old harbour, where, lining the cliff edge, is a TEA-GARDEN. Here you can sip tea and admire the view while you recover from the walk. Back down the steps, head for a closer look at the OLD HARBOUR. No expense has been spared to restore and refurbish it, and it is now a lively, popular social centre.

It would seem that wherever the Emperor Hadrian went visiting, the populace felt moved to build him a gate; Antalya was no exception. You can see the impressive remains of this THREE-ARCHED PORTAL, erected in 130 AD, lying somewhat below today's ground level on ATATÜRK CADDESI.

For a break from the noise and bustle of the city, take a stroll in the KARAALI PARKI. The Antalyans take a special pride in this flower-filled oasis, and there are wonderful views of the sea and the surrounding mountains. Here you will also see the remains of the HIDIRLIK KÜLESI, a squat, round, Roman tower. No-one seems particularly clear as to what it was designed for, although the base was probably a tomb and the upper part, a later addition, used as a lighthouse.

In the main square on CUMHURIYET CADDESI there is a wonderfully over the top EQUESTRIAN STATUE OF ATATÜRK. From this street you can hop on a bus or a *dolmuş* heading westwards to get to the ANTALYA MUSEUM.

As Turkish museums go, the Antalya museum is really quite good. The exhibits are well displayed and most are marked clearly, but with somewhat limited information in English. But it's a cool airy building, and a great relief from the sweltering heat of an Antalya summer afternoon. There are halls filled with Greek and Roman sculptures, endless tombs and intricately carved sarcophagi, mosaics, an ethnographic collection and exhibits from the Stone Age.

There are numerous good places to eat in Antalya, but for a cheap meal and for atmosphere, head for the centre of the city, to the intersection of ATATÜRK and CUMHURIYET CADDESI; here you will find a narrow street packed with little RESTAU-RANTS. In some you can eat on the roof or sit amidst the bustle and noise at tables packed together in the street itself. None of these restaurants serves alcohol but there are Turkish versions of off-licences at either end of the street, where you can buy your particular poison. The food is chiefly *kebaps*, either with yoghourt or tomato sauce served with salad and bread. It's cheap, tasty and fun.

Past the Atatürk statue on CUMHURIYET CADDESI, heading a little further west, there are a couple of restaurants perched on the edge of the cliff. Try and get a ringside seat on a moonlit night; wonderful views unless you happen to suffer from vertigo. There are still more restaurants in the Karaali Parkı and some excellent ones in the old harbour.

There are two main BEACHES on either side of the city. KONYAALTI PLAJI is to the west of the bay. Pebble, rather than sand, it is marred by a string of ramshackle bars and restaurants. LARA PLAJI, to the east, is about 15 km from the centre. If you don't have a car you can take a *dolmuş*. The service is quick, frequent and cheap. All along the road leading to Lara there are HOTELS, PANSIYONS and RESTAURANTS. It is generally a better idea to stay out here rather than in Antalya. Lara has a long, sandy beach: you have to pay a small entrance fee.

On the way to Lara stop and look at the LOWER DÜDEN WATERFALLS plunging 50 m over the cliff-face to the sea. Further up the river are the UPPER DÜDEN WATERFALLS set in a small, landscaped park. Here, a series of falls tumble into little lagoons. If you don't mind getting very damp, you can walk right under the falls by means of a series of passageways cut into the rock. The surface is very slippery, so watch your step.

TERMESSOS

When Alexander the Great rampaged across Anatolia in 333 BC, he met with little resistance anywhere, and when he did, it was easily quashed. Not so in the case of TERMESSOS; one look at its impregnable position, perched a dizzy 1,524 m up on a craggy peak, and the invincible Alexander decided not to risk blotting his hitherto perfect copy-book and withdrew.

In antiquity, this mountain region was known as Pisidia, and Termessos was its most powerful city. The Pisidians were a fierce, warlike bunch who showed little inclination to knuckle under to the Romans. Indeed the Romans took the line of least resistance with the Termessians, and signed a treaty with them, granting them extensive autonomy. The Termessians flaunted their unique position by not including images of the Roman Emperor on their coins.

The RUINS OF TERMESSOS have not as yet been excavated, and it might be better if it was to remain that way. It is a wildly romantic spot, the air is clear and sharp and the profusion of wild flowers and butterflies amidst olive trees and mountain pine, make this one of the most beautiful sites in Turkey. There are no souvenir shops or ramshackle cafes at the entrance to the site, and although it is included on coach tour itineraries, it does not get as crowded as other more accessible sites. If you go at the extremes of the day, you stand a very good chance of being alone in the midst of all this exhilarating splendour.

Leave Antalya by the Burdur-Isparta road, turning off for KORKUTELI after about 12 km. Follow this road until you see signs to the left for the site. Follow the rough track, about 9 km, until you reach a clearing where you must abandon your car and continue on foot. If you don't have a car you can arrange for a private taxi tour, but make sure you agree the price before you set off. If you take a *dolmuş* or a bus from Antalya you will be dropped at the end of the road leading up to the site and will have a very long, tiring hike before you reach the ruins of Termessos.

To explore the city thoroughly involves a considerable scramble but much can be seen by making small, quite well-trodden detours to the left of the main pathway. The major attractions are signposted.

In the parking area you can see the remains of the GATE OF HADRIAN before you start the stiff climb up the path towards the NECROPOLIS. On your way up you will see the overgrown, but still impressive remains of the GYMNASIUM, followed by the most stunning sight in Termessos – the THEATRE. If you are spending any length of time in Turkey, you will see a lot of theatres. Many are better preserved and many are bigger and more elaborate; but none has such an awe-inspiring, dramatic setting. Seating 4,500 people, the theatre seems suspended on the edge of the mountain. The performers and the wild animals must have had their work cut out competing with the view for the attention of the audience.

Close by are the overgrown, tumbledown remains of a smaller theatre, the ODEON, used for musical performances and as a council chamber. Clustered round the odeon are the collapsed remains of a series of TEMPLES. Continue up the steep pathway to explore the Necropolis. Here, earthquakes and grave robbers have taken their toll. Huge stone tombs tumble down the mountainside in chaotic profusion. You can clamber amongst them and examine the reliefs and carved inscriptions. These inscriptions are not only tributes to those buried within, but warnings to would-be grave robbers of the penalties imposed for desecration. Watch out for snakes if you plan to scramble deep into the undergrowth.

At the very top you will reach the FIRETOWER, from where the fire watchman keeps his lonely vigil, whilst contemplating one of the most breathtaking views in Turkey.

Downhill all the way now, with a detour to the left of the path to visit another tomb, purported to be the burial place of Alcetas. After the death of Alexander the Great, when his vast empire was parcelled out to his three generals, one of them, Antigonus, had ambitions in Asia beyond his inheritance. Opposed by Alcetas, who was supported by the Pisidians, the two met in battle, and Alcetas was soundly defeated. Retreating to Termessos, he was pursued by Antigonus, who threatened to destroy the city unless Alcetas was handed over for punishment. The city was divided. The elders were all for taking the line of least resistance, and handing over Alcetas. The younger men refused. In secret the elders hatched a plot with Antigonus. The general's troops were to appear to withdraw, and while the young Termessians were in hot pursuit, the elders would deliver the hapless Alcetas, dead or alive, to Antigonus. The plan worked, but Alcetas, getting wind of the plot, committed suicide. His body was delivered to Antigonus who heaped indignities on it before abandoning it to decompose on the mountainside. The young Termessians, cursing the elders, retrieved the body and gave it a hero's burial.

Carved into the rock you can see a mounted warrior, presumably depicting Alcetas in his final battle against Antigonus.

ASPENDOS

ASPENDOS is about halfway between Antalya and Side to the north of the main road. Follow the bank of the KÖPRÜ RIVER, passing a beautiful SELJUK BRIDGE beside the ruins of a ROMAN BRIDGE; from the size of the ruins you can see how enormous the arch would have been. The river is badly silted now, but it used to be navigable by large craft as far as Aspendos.

Continuing upriver for 3 km, you see the great high-arched AQUEDUCT striding across the valley. Built in the second century AD, the whole thing is believed to be the gift of one Tiberius Claudius Italicus to the city – two million denarii. Such charitable bequests were not uncommon in the cities of the time, and serve as a good illustration of how wealthy one could become in the days of the Roman Empire.

The city's main claim to fame is its THEATRE, undoubtedly the best preserved Roman theatre in the world; some of the restoration work is a little obvious and probably horrifies the purists, but what you see today is what the citizens of Aspendos would have seen in 200 AD, when the two brothers, Curtius Crispinus and Curtius Auspicatus, gave the city its theatre. The well preserved high stage-building was typical of Roman theatres, where the action would take place on a stage, with the stage-building as a background. In Greek theatres, the action generally took place in the orchestra, and the backdrop would be the distant hills or sea or whatever happened to be visible from the auditorium.

SELGE

If you have plenty of time to spare, you might like to make the long detour off the main Antalya-Side road to SELGE. It is not as spectacular as the cities of the Pamphylian Plain, but its situation in spectacular mountain scenery makes it worth the trouble.

From Aspendos, go back to the main road, turn east, then after 3 km, head north up to BEŞKONAK; follow the valley of the ancient Eurymedon up for about 30 km; it's a rough road and a steep climb as far as Beşkonak, and after that, just a track for 15 km up to SELGE at 914 m. Set high in the hills of PISIDIA, the city is not unlike Termessos, though Selge is more difficult to reach and built on a very much smaller scale. According to the geographer Strabo, the surrounding country was so tortuous that it 'protected the town from ever – even once – becoming subject to another people'. The inhabitants were by all accounts prosperous, well-travelled and civilised – 'the most noteworthy of the Pisidians'.

PERGE

Perge is north of the main coast road 15 km east of Antalya. First you come to the THEATRE – not quite as grand as at Aspendos or Side, but nonetheless impressive and largely intact. It has some fine carved reliefs on the stage-building, including a chariot drawn by lions and a head of Medusa.

Across the track is the STADIUM, better preserved here than at the other cities. Athletics and sports played an important part in Greek and Roman culture; every major city would hold its own games; there would have been over 100 different major events every year around the Mediterranean during the first 300 years AD. There would have even been professional sportsmen, who would turn up in hundreds, whenever a particular city was holding its Games, in quest of trophies and valuable prizes.

The best part of the city is the centre, within the walls; enter by the old MAIN GATE with its great circular towers, part of the original Hellenistic fortifications. Continue north up what remains of the colonnaded MAIN STREET. This magnificent street was 20 m wide with broad covered galleries running down either side, their wooden roofs supported by twin rows of white marble columns; in the centre was a channel 2 m wide, which would have been full of clear flowing water, cascading over the weirs – as much a decorative feature as part of the city's water-system. Altogether, a highly civilised shopping street.

The huge PUBLIC BATHS to the west of the main street are sufficiently intact so that you can see each separate room and, in particular, the HEATING SYSTEM beneath – a massive cistern supported by brick arches, for the circulation of hot water and steam.

Perge was known throughout the Ancient World for the magnificence of its TEMPLE OF ARTEMIS, but curiously enough, though trenches have been dug and dozens of learned theories postulated, there is no sign of it today, not even the foundations.

In common with the other cities of Pamphylia, Perge fell into decline with the Empire of Rome, and took such a battering from the raids of the Arabs in the seventh century, that there was little left but a small town when the Ottomans came to power. Under the Turks it declined still further, and there were no further settlements. This accounts for the city's good state of preservation.

SIDE

SIDE lies at the southern end of the PLAINS OF PAMPHYLIA; here the Taurus Mountains withdraw from the shore for a stretch of some 80 km, leaving a fertile plain, more prosperous and habitable than the rocky coasts of Lycia to the west, or 'Rough Cilicia' to the east.

The city was probably founded around 1000 BC by some of the 'mixed multitude of peoples' who wandered into the East after the fall of Troy. Legend has it that as soon as these settlers arrived at the peninsula of Side, they began to speak a tongue quite unknown to themselves or anybody else, forgetting their native Greek. It's a fanciful story, and it would be easy to dismiss it as nonsense – but Side did, for a long time, have a language quite unrelated to Greek or any of the languages of Anatolia, and inscriptions have been found dating from 300 BC, in a language that nobody, as yet, has been able to make head or tail of.

Side is the best preserved of the five ancient cities of Pamphylia. The others are Antalya, Aspendos, Sillyum and Perge. The ruins cover a large area, most of which has been excavated in the last 50 years. It is certainly one of the finest Classical sites of Turkey, with the great advantage that you can stay here and wander alone through the ruins, after the guides and their coach-parties have gone.

Some 70 km east of Antalya, turn south off the main coast road at MANAVGAT and continue another 6 km to Side. The cotton-fields beside the road are cluttered with Roman ruins, mostly of the AQUEDUCT that brought the city's water from high up the Manavgat River, 30 km away. To the west, a road leads to a long sand BEACH and a mass of HOTELS, CAMPSITES and RESTAURANTS. Straight on, the fragments of ancient civilisation become more and more concentrated, until you turn a corner and see right before your eyes, the CITY GATE, the NYMPHAEUM and the great arched semi-circle of the ROMAN THEATRE.

Start with the theatre, which is the finest building here, and one of the largest and best preserved theatres in Turkey. Built by the Romans in the second century AD, it is unusual and especially impressive in that it was built on flat ground, whereas other theatres in Asia Minor take advantage of the sides of hills. To support the higher part of the Auditorium therefore, a great semi-circular building was constructed on massive arched piers; inside, runs a vaulted gallery which would have been lined with shops and store-rooms. The Cavea, or Auditorium which rises above these galleries, could seat 20,000 spectators.

The Orchestra in the centre was surrounded by a wall, 1.8 m high, which would have protected the spectators from the attentions of the wild beasts used in gladiatorial combats. It has also been suggested that this wall was waterproofed, so the Orchestra could be flooded, and naval battles enacted – though it seems to me that they must have been very small naval battles.

The GATE beside the Theatre was not the city's main gate; it would have been a TRIUMPHAL ARCH surmounted by a statue of the Emperor-God in a chariot with four horses. As the city declined in the fourth century AD, the population dwindled and resources became scarce, so the size of the city was reduced by building a new city wall across the narrow neck of the peninsula. The former Inner City Gate, with a smaller archway built inside the main arch to improve its defensive qualities, now served as the Main Gate.

Beside this gate is the NYMPHAEUM, originally built in another part of the city as a monument to the Emperor Vespasian, but moved here and turned into a fountain when the city was reduced in size. This elegant monument formerly contained several statues; the one of Hermes is now in the Museum.

The MUSEUM is housed in a converted and restored ROMAN BATH by the main gate; the best of the statues, sarcophagi, tombs and other finds are now protected in here; it is one of the finest archaeological museums in Turkey.

The great open space opposite the Museum is the AGORA – marketplace. It would have been surrounded by two rows of the columns that now lie tumbled on the ground, forming a gallery, roofed with timber and lined with shops. This area would have been the main meeting-place of the town.

Wandering around on this lovely site, by the sea, you will come across many more impressive ruins; the TEMPLES OF ATHENA, APOLLO, DIONYSIUS and MEN (Moon God), the BATHS, a LIBRARY, BASILICAS and a NECROPOLIS.

The inhabitants of the modern village are said to be a displaced population from Crete, settled here when the Ottoman Empire was disbanded at the turn of the century. Anyway, they have made a virtue out of necessity by building a road over the old Roman colonnaded street – to the consternation of archaeologists – and establishing a pleasant little fishing village and tourist haven. It is very popular with Turks and foreigners alike, and deservedly so, for it has everything you could want from a Mediterranean village: jasmine, bougainvillea and vines; wooden fishing boats bringing in every conceivable type of fish; well-proportioned, attractive villas, some of which are PANSIYONS with pretty gardens; BEACHES; incomparable ruins.

There are plenty of good HOTELS and RESTAURANTS, modest PANSIYONS and tourist facilities such as car-hire and coach-tours of the cities of Pamphylia.

ALANYA

What is known of the ancient history of ALANYA is patchy. The Cilician coast was the haunt of pirates, and Alanya, ancient Coracesium, was their headquarters. They were left much to their own devices until Rome decided to put an end to their activities, and sent Pompey to deal with them. The pirate fleet was destroyed in a fierce sea battle off Coracesium in 67 BC.

Mark Antony, besotted with Cleopatra, made her a present of Coracesium and the land surrounding it; an extremely practical little gift, for the area was densely forested and the wood was just what the lady needed to build her fleet.

Few details are known of the history of Alanya and the region until the rise to power of the Seljuk Turks. From his base in Konya, Sultan Alaeddin Keykubad I had his eye on Alanya, currently under the control of an Armenian governor. In 1221 he attacked. It was not an easy task, for the fortress was virtually impregnable. One unlikely, but amusing story goes as follows: Keykubad had been laying siege to the castle for some time, with no sign of submission from the occupants. Any attempt at an attack from all sides would have been suicidal; the sheer face of the promontory on which the fortress is built was only negotiable for goats – not soldiers. The sultan therefore ordered that all the goats from the surrounding area be brought to him. In the dead of night flaming torches were tied to the horns of the unfortunate beasts and they were stampeded up the cliffside. Under the impression that the castle was being attacked by thousands of troops, the commander promptly opened the gates and surrendered – presumably to the goats.

Whatever his strategy, Keykubad took control and renamed the town Alaiye making it his winter quarters. Alanya flourished during the Seljuk period, but after their decline, the town sank into relative obscurity. The Ottomans disregarded it, and it was not until quite recently that any interest or investment was directed to this area. Now it is a busy modern town, with tourism a thriving industry. BEACHES on both sides of the town are excellent, there are plenty of RESTAURANTS and CAFES strung out along the waterfront road leading to the harbour, and the streets are full of shops offering carpets, leather, copper and jewellery and other Turkish handicrafts.

The old town straggles up and around a huge 244 m rocky promontory, magnificently crowned by an impressive SELJUK FORTRESS. It's a long, steep walk to the top, so if you go on foot, avoid the hottest part of the day.

At the foot of the road leading up to the fortress is the KIZILKULE or Red Tower. Built by Keykubad to protect the harbour, this octagonal tower was restored in the early 1950s. Close by the Red Tower you will find the old Seljuk SHIPYARD (*Tersane*), a series of vaulted galleries, five in total, flanked by another tower which was used as an arsenal.

As you go up the winding road towards the fortress you will pass through the original MAIN GATE of the outer wall – a wall that is over 8 km long and took twelve years to build. On your way to the fortress on the summit you will see further remains of Seljuk buildings. A BEDESTEN and CARAVANSERAI, the SÜLEYMANIYE MOSQUE, and a building known as the AKSEBE TÜRBESI, used both as a tomb and as a mosque. All these buildings lie in the residential area of the old fortress town, known as EHMEDEK within the second fortification wall. By the time you get to the summit and enter through the crenellated third wall to the fortress proper, you will begin to understand why it was so impregnable. One look down over the precipitous cliff face from the viewing platforms inside, and you will be convinced. In the north-west corner is an area known as ADAM ATACAĞI, literally translated it means 'place from which men may be thrown'; from here, it seems, condemned criminals were summarily despatched over the edge to meet their death on the savage rocks below.

Within the fortress the only well preserved building is a small BYZANTINE CHURCH. Inside you can still see patches of frescoes on the walls. Aside from the church, there is little to see, other than a stunning view of the town and the coastline fringed by the Taurus mountains. Cold drinks and tea can be bought to slake your thirst before you walk back down.

On the western side of the peninsula you will find Alanya's small MUSEUM, displaying numerous finds from the area. Nearby is the DAMLATAŞ CAVE. If you suffer from rheumatism or bronchial problems, and you have plenty of time on your hands, this is the place to go. A combination of radioactive elements and high humidity, around 95 per cent, with a temperature of about 24°C is purported to be beneficial if you spend long enough inside.

You can take a boat trip from the harbour by the Red Tower, which will take you round the promontory to see the LOVERS' CAVE, the PIRATES' CAVE and the PHOSPHORESCENT CAVE. Included in the tour is a quick glimpse of the beach where Cleopatra supposedly used to swim. The round trip takes about an hour, and while it is certainly a pleasant way to pass the time, the caves don't live up to their evocative names and Cleopatra's beach is, at best, uninspiring.

ANAMUR

East of Alanya, the road continues on the flat for 50 km to GAZIPAŞA, a place that's less interesting than it sounds; thereafter the road forsakes the flat coastal plain with its sweeping beaches, and takes to the hills for the hair-raising drive to ANAMUR.

Anamur is a small town in the centre of one of the fertile deltas that here and there emerge from the Taurus Mountains. It's pleasant enough, with a few restaurants and hotels, but nothing to see in the town itself. The best place to stay is on the ANAMUR İSKELE, the seaside village that has grown up beside the town's jetty, 3 km south of Anamur proper. The quietest PANSIYONS are in the fields behind the beach away from the thump and beat of the beach disco. Here, you can eat fish at one of the many seafront RESTAURANTS, and walk along the beach to visit the great CRUSADER CASTLE to the east. This huge castle, overgrown and lonely, with the sea beating endlessly on its walls, is almost intact; you can stride on the ramparts or stumble along the dark passages within the massive walls. Its remarkable state of preservation is due largely to the fact that it was used by the Ottomans up to the end of the nineteenth century. It is believed to have been built in the twelfth century by the Armenians, who held this part of the coast at that time, as Lesser Armenia. It's 40 minutes walk along the beach, and a ferryride across the river, costing just a few lira.

Up the other way, but a much longer walk – two hours or so – is the ANCIENT CITY OF ANAMURYUM; take a *dolmuş* from the town if you're not up to the walk. Here you have a lovely beach with nobody about, and another huge MEDIEVAL FORTRESS, looking just like a castle should. Behind is a fabulous ruined ROMAN CITY with colonnaded streets, triumphal gates, temples, baths and fountains scattered amongst the oleanders and fig-trees. The Ministry of Tourism and Culture has not got its hands on the site yet, so it's yours for the taking – a beautiful spot, with the high mountains of the Taurus rising behind.

Still heading east, the road climbs back up onto the corniche and winds its way through pine-clad mountains, with breath-taking views of the sea glimpsed through the banana plantations below. A 2½ hour drive takes you to SILIFKE.

SILIFKE

Little frequented by tourists, SILIFKE is small and quiet. There are nevertheless some splendid things to see in the area.

The town itself is agreeable, with a few modest HOTELS, RESTAURANTS with tables in the street, and surprises, like the ruined TEMPLE OF JUPITER, by the road to the bus-station. One perfect Classical column stands proudly, while the others lie tumbled among exquisite Roman friezes and carvings. On the hill dominating the town are the ruins of a mighty CRUSADER CASTLE, with much of its walls and towers still intact; climb up in the evening and take tea in the tea-garden or eat in the KALE RESTAURANT.

Crossing the GÖKSU RIVER is a fine ROMAN STONE BRIDGE, to the east of which is Silifke's TOURIST OFFICE. I mention this because this is, along with Bursa, the most energetic and interested Tourist Office in Turkey; it is staffed by people with a boundless enthusiasm for their town and its surroundings. They don't have the resources to produce the multi-coloured nonsense you are given in the main tourist destinations, so they produce their own, doing all their own research and printing pamphlets on a decrepit machine with a handle. These they give away, or sell for a pittance, and they contain more useful information than anything else you will find in Turkey.

They will suggest you go to UZUNCABURÇ. Uzuncaburç may be a poor fish compared to Ephesus with its vastness and grandeur; but its great advantage is that the only other visitors will be goats and butterflies. Take a *dolmuş* in the morning. For 30 km to the north-east of Silifke, you climb easily through beautiful Mediterranean mountain scenery, the air drenched with the scent of pine, figs and herbs. Soon, Roman tombs start to appear among the woods in a matter of fact sort of way; then you are up on the cool hill, 915 m high, at the village of Uzuncaburç. Here, twined among the houses and cobbled lanes of a Turkish village, is the ruined Hellenistic city of OLBIA or DIOCAESAREA. It was probably founded by Seleucus, one of Alexander the Great's most able generals, in 300 BC, the same year that he founded Antioch.

The eastern gate of the city, the PORTICUS, has five columns still standing, surmounted by the remains of a frieze, supported on beautiful Corinthian capitals. Step through the porticus and walk along the colonnaded street, past the NYMPHAEUM (fountain), until you come to the great TEMPLE OF ZEUS on the left; the 30 standing columns are all that is left of a temple built in 295 BC. Leave the temple and go straight across the crossroads to the TRIUMPHAL GATE of the city. This magnificent, perfectly proportioned monumental gate was constructed round about the birth of Christ; no mortar was used, it relied only upon the perfect cut of the massive limestone blocks.

There is a TEA-GARDEN in the village, and a very basic RESTAURANT; there are also many more ruins – a curious FORTIFIED TOWER, from which the village gets its name, a THEATRE, NECROPOLIS and TEMPLE OF TYCHE. To return to Silifke, there is one bus a day, and several *dolmuşes*; but failing all else, you can start walking – you won't walk far without the offer of a lift.

Only 10 km west of Silifke is the little port and seaside resort of TAŞUCU, with a good bathing BEACH and daily boats to KYRENIA in CYPRUS.

Follow the coast 25 km north-east from Silifke, to reach the village of KIZKALESI – the 'Maiden's Castle'. Some 500 m offshore is a fine MEDIEVAL CASTLE – hence the name; you can take a boat, or swim out, for the sea is very shallow for a long way. There is a rather feeble legend about this place: the King of Corycus (for that was the name of the city here), having heard from a soothsayer that his dearly beloved daughter would die of a snakebite, sent her to a snake-less island, where he built her a castle, and provided her with a lifestyle of unimaginable opulence. One day, a fruiterer appeared in a boat, and sold the maiden a basket of fruit – and what do you think was in the basket? Well, a snake, of course; and it proceeded to bite the princess on the finger, whereupon she died. It's not a bad legend really; it's just that the same legend is told of every single offshore island, rock or inaccessible tower in Turkey.

Opposite Kızkalesi, on the shore, is another MEDIEVAL CASTLE; together, they made the sea-fortifications of the ancient city of Corycus, the ruins of which are scattered over the hills surrounding the village of Kızkalesi. Corycus was a considerable city from well before Roman times, up to the Middle Ages, as can be seen from the Pagan and Christian religious and secular remains. The city declined in the later Middle Ages; today the village is enjoying a revival as a noisy and bouncy holiday resort for Turkish 'Gastarbeiters'. The village, with its mass of PANSIYONS, RESTAURANTS and souvenir-shops, is right on the BEACH; the sea is warm and clean. You could well spend days here, wandering among the ruins and cooling off from time to time in the sea.

The village of NARLIKUYU is 7 km towards Silifke, and has the smallest MUSEUM you are ever likely to see; it stands on the site of a ROMAN BATH, and it has one solitary exhibit – the mosaic floor of the bath. The mosaic, which is astonishingly well preserved, depicts 'The Three Graces'; a delightful and rather erotic subject that frequently appears in pictures or sculptures in Classical Art. Three naked, half divine beauties dance among flowers and appreciative songbirds – '...three fair-cheeked Graces, from whose eyes, as they danced, flowed love and unnerved the limps', runs a curious translation from the Roman poet, Hesiod. The mosaic is acclaimed as one of the most beautiful examples of this type of decoration to be seen anywhere today.

The CORYCIAN CAVES, *Cennet* and *Cehennem* (Heaven and Hell) are 2 km inland. *Cehennem* is a deep and awful pit, with concave sides, like an 'oubliette', where legend has it that the Giant Typhon was imprisoned. It is really no more than an impressive, horrible hole in the ground, plunging to 130 m. *Cennet*, on the other hand, is more agreeable; a steep path and steps, part ancient, part modern, lead down through fig-trees and flowers to a simple ARMENIAN CHURCH in the depth of a deep cleft in the earth; birds sing and it's delightfully cool and green. Here, young boys wait to guide you with paraffin-lamps, into the black depths below the church; the steps are damp and slippery, the huge cave dark and icy-cold; your guide with his light, will be swinging gaily ahead, rushing along to get back for the next group of tourists. Don't let him hurry you, for the cave is beautiful in a sombre way; there is a forest of stalactites above you in the gloom, and fantastic pinnacles rise to meet them. At the very bottom of the cave is a rock wall, behind which you can hear the roaring of an underground stream. A spring of clear water is said to impart wisdom to whomsoever drinks from it; it appears to be quite ineffective! Now you must climb back from the cool depths to the searing heat of the Mediterranean sun.

Don't forget the village of Narlikuyu itself. It's a tiny village in the crook of a bay; nothing more than a cobbled square, shaded by plane trees. By the sea are several FISH RESTAURANTS, their terraces lapped by the water; near where the fishing-boats beach is a small HOTEL with a vine-shaded terrace. The water in the bay is perfectly clear and full of fish; it also has the unique property of being ice-cold on the surface, yet warm below. This has apparently baffled scientists for years; but it may have something to do with the underground river in the cave. This village, which has a population of about 50 people, is a wonderful place to stay for exploring the area.

EAST OF SILIFKE

From Silifke it's 1½ hours by road to MERSIN; the road runs past miles of fast-growing seaside towns with good sandy beaches and fields of oranges and lemons behind. There are banana plantations too, for the climate is very hot and humid here.

Mersin is the principal port for eastern Turkey, but it lacks the fascination of other port-cities, simply because it is less than 100 years old, and the harbour is entirely artificial. There are moves afoot to develop the town as a tourist capital, serving the long line of resorts to the west, but at the moment it has little of interest.

You would expect TARSUS, the birthplace of St Paul, to be crammed with ancient monuments; alas, it is just a dull modern city and hardly worth a visit.

ADANA, an hour from Mersin, is the fourth largest city in Turkey, with a booming economy based on the fertile agricultural plain around it. The city has little to delight the tourist, but what there is, lies within five minutes walk of the *Otogar*, so you could 'do' the town if you happen to be waiting for a bus connection. The BRIDGE that crosses the SEYHAN RIVER was built in the reign of Hadrian, and, with a few modifications, has survived virtually intact. Right next to the bus-station is the ADANA MUSEUM, with a fine collection of Hittite statuary and stoneware, Roman sarcophagi and Turkish nomads' artefacts.

At the junction 100 km further east, where the road to Iskenderun and Antakya leaves the East Anatolia road, stands the gloomy castle of TOPRAKKALE, guarding the pass to the Plains of Issos. From here, it's an hour south to Iskenderun.

ANTAKYA

With the death of Alexander the Great and the fragmentation of his empire, Seleucus, one of his generals, founded a city in 300 BC on the sea at the mouth of the River Orontes. The city was well placed to control the important routes from Syria and Iraq into Anatolia; he called it, modestly, Seleucia, as he called the other eight cities he was to found. The city prospered and, by the time the Romans conquered it in 64 AD, it was an important centre of trade and culture. It became the third city of the Roman Empire, with 500,000 inhabitants and a reputation for opulence and refined debauchery.

Christianity came early to ANTIOCH, as it became known, for St Peter spent several years preaching in the city, and soon there was a strong Christian community with churches and religious foundations. Security and peace never stayed long in this contentious part of the world; on several occasions the city was flattened by earthquakes and stricken by plagues, with terrible loss of life; and it was a constant victim of conquerors – Romans, Persians, Arabs, Seljuk Turks, Crusaders, Mamelukes and finally Ottomans. Surprisingly enough, a flourishing city grew, with a highly developed culture and great wealth, a rival even to Athens in the affairs of the ancient world.

You would hardly believe this, visiting modest Antakya today. The town is cut in two by the ASI RIVER (Orontes of old); to the east is the old town with a colourful and lively market area and tiny mosques on every corner. On the west side is the new town, laid out with wide avenues and plenty of trees and parks; if it doesn't look typically Turkish, it's because the French, who held Antakya and the surrounding area after the First World War, constructed most of the town. By the bridge is the MOSAIC MUSEUM.

The HATAY, the bit that sticks out of Turkey at the eastern end of the south coast, is rich in archaeological remains, mostly Roman or Hellenic, but with many sites dating as far back as the Hittites. The best of the finds, and in particular the wonderful mosaics found in the Roman houses at nearby Daphne, are displayed in the museum. The mosaics you see here are probably the finest examples ever produced; for this form of decoration only enjoyed a brief popularity. By the end of the fifth century AD it had died out altogether. Depictions of the gods feature heavily, as well as allegorical tableaux of the Four Seasons; then there are a number of humorous and mildly lewd scenes which help to remind us of the human side of the Romans. The simplest works are merely geometrical designs. The subtlety, delicacy and skill with which this odd medium is handled is very impressive and increases our respect for the civilisation which, so long ago, attained such a peak of artistic excellence. You could spend a whole day in this marvellous museum.

The GROTTO OF ST PETER is 2 km east of the city. Here the saint is supposed to have preached. Said by some to be the very first Christian church, it has a simple altar and a statue of St Peter; the curious façade was added by the Crusaders, who felt that the cave wasn't sufficiently splendid. On 29 June, St Peter's Day, a service is still held here.

Unfortunately little remains of the great walls of Antioch, which, allied to the city's impressive natural defences, made it one of the most formidable bastions of the ancient East.

On the sea, 30 km west of Antakya, is the ancient harbour of the city, at the mouth of the Orontes. SELEUCIA PIERIA was one of the most important ports in the Mediterranean under the Romans; but it silted up, so little remains to be seen today, except for the astonishing tunnel bored through the mountain by the Romans. It was built to divert the seasonal floodwaters of the river, and so prevent the harbour from silting up. It was a nice idea ... for connoisseurs of monumental engineering feats, this is worth seeing.

HARBIYE, the site of the ancient pleasure-park of Daphne, where the mosaics come from, lies about 8 km south of Antakya. There's little of historical interest left, but it's a lovely spot for a stroll or a picnic, and it has some good little RESTAURANTS.

Up the coast to the north, 50 km away, is ISKENDERUN, formerly Alexandretta. It's a very busy port in a beautiful bay, ringed with mountains – a wonderful setting; unfortunately that's all it has to offer and, apart from the seafront promenade, with its palm-trees, tea-gardens and spectacular view, the town is dull, and contains no notable buildings. Should you unaccountably be washed up on this shore, you'd be better off in ARSUZ, 30 km to the south. It is a fishing village with a perfect sandy BEACH.

C·H·A·P·T·E·R· 7

Inland Central

KONYA

Konya is worth visiting for two things: SELJUK ARCHITECTURE and the TOMB OF MEVLANA CELALEDDIN RUMI, the founder of the 'Whirling Dervishes'. Konya, Iconium to the Romans, first achieved prominence in the twelfth and thirteenth centuries, as the capital of the flourishing SELJUK dynasty; it is from this period that the best of the city dates. The Seljuks, however, had many enemies; the early development of their civilisation and culture was hampered by the constant attentions of the Crusaders and their offshoots; at the close of the thirteenth century they fell to the Mongols; hard on the heels of the Mongols came the Karamanoğulları, another of the powerful Turkic tribes vying for ascendancy in Anatolia. They held the city until 1467, when it was taken by the Ottomans, who didn't show much interest, letting the city fall into decline. It only really recovered with the arrival of the railway at the end of the nineteenth century.

Take for a starting point the ALAEDDIN TEPE, the hill at the end of HÜKÜMET CADDESI, the main street. The sad ruins under the curious concrete canopy are the remains of a SELJUK PALACE, of which you can make out nothing but a few blackened stones. More worthy of inspection is the ALAEDDIN CAMII on the hill, built in 1220 by Alaeddin Keykubad, the sultan who presided over the military and cultural zenith of the Seljuks. The mosque is quite different from the other mosques you will see elsewhere in Turkey. The inside is a huge low prayer-hall – no high dome – just a wooden ceiling over simple unadorned brick arches, supported by 42 columns, some plain, some boldly carved with the typical Seljuk knot motif. All the columns were removed from earlier Roman or Byzantine buildings. An intricately carved wooden *minber* attests to the skill of Seljuk craftsmen.

For a good example of more astonishing stone and wood carving, go round the back of the hill (west) to the INCE MINARE MEDRESE (Slender Minaret), now a museum. Look at the stone-carving round the door – it's the finest you'll see, with

Typical elaborate Seljuk portal

its wonderful knotted stone and the intricacy of its geometric and floral patterns. Unfortunately the 'Slender Minaret' of the name was knocked off by lightning; it too has some fine carving on the base. Inside is the MUSEUM OF WOOD AND STONE CARVING.

Another portal which must rate with that of the Ince Minare as the finest work the Seljuks ever produced, is the KARATAY MEDRESE, on the north side of the hill. Here are scriptural texts and complex geometrical patterns carved into marble. Unfortunately it's not easy to admire this one because it's right on the edge of a busy road. Inside is the MUSEUM OF CERAMIC ART. The interior of the building, formerly a theological college, is itself a riot of beautiful blue tiles. In the centre of the room is a pool; display-cases contain a collection of exquisite tiles and pottery. If you still have the appetite for one more fine Seljuk portal, the SIRÇALI MEDRESE MUSEUM (Funerary Art), is just a couple of blocks to the south of the hill, down SIRÇALI MEDRESE SOKAĞI. Keep going down this street for the SAHIP ATA CAMII, with another, different portal, and the ARCHAEO-LOGY MUSEUM.

Going east down the main street, towards the MEVLANA MUSEUM, you pass on the right the IPLIKÇI CAMII, Konya's oldest mosque (1202), rather plain and dull.

After the square, turn right down ISTANBUL CADDESI, to get to the AZIZIYE CAMII. This one comes as something of a shock to the practised observer of Ottoman mosques, for, built in 1872, during a period of decadence and stagnation in monumental architecture – as well as in everything else – new influences were clutched like straws; the result is a unique Baroque mosque. Have a look at it with its extravagantly ornamented minarets, and lively interior decoration, and wonder where Turkish mosque-building would have gone, had this caught on.

Further east, at the end of the main street is the SELIMIYE CAMII. This is a fine Ottoman mosque, reminiscent of the great age of building in Istanbul in the sixteenth century. Next door is the Mevlana Museum.

The MEVLANA MUSEUM is one of the holy places of Islam, for the influence of the Mevlevi sect was, and still is, very powerful throughout all the lands of the Ottoman Empire. Pilgrims come from far away to worship at the tomb of their spiritual leader. Indeed it is a moving sight to see devout old men and women (in the thirteenth century Mevlana pas-sionately advocated equal status for women) worshipping quietly in corners of the museum amongst the swirling throng of visitors. The teachings of the sect, set out in verse form in the MESNEVI and the DIVAN-I-KEBIR , are religious tolerance, the brotherhood of *all* men before God, gentleness, humility and charity. The Mevlana preached that all men are born free – he himself kept no slaves or concubines and was married to one woman all his life.

> *Come, come again, whoever, whatever you may be, come*
> *Heathen, fire-worshipper, sinful of idolatory, come*
> *Come even if you have sinned a hundred times*
> *Ours is not the portal of despair and misery, come*

The museum itself is really worth a visit. At weekends and religious festivals it gets very crowded, and so great is the press of the throng, that your feet barely touch the ground. Try and go early on a weekday morning, and wander in peace into the holy room where the Mevlana and many of his disciples lie in their richly shrouded sarcophagi, surmounted by their turbans. Other rooms contain the most exquisitely illuminated Korans, religious musical instruments, carpets, silks and wall-hangings, and a mass of finely crafted religious artefacts. The exhibition halls were formerly the monastery and religious school of the Dervishes and their cells surround the marble courtyard with its central fountain. Capping the *medrese* is a unique conical tower, faced with bright blue and turquoise tiles.

The 'Sema', or dance of the Whirling Dervishes, takes place in December at the museum. To the Mevlevi (followers of Mevlana) music and the dance represent a channel of spiritual communion with God. The upturned palm receives the gift of enlightenment from Heaven, while the downturned palm distributes it upon the earth. The dance is intricate, and in each

Whirling Dervishes

slightest motion, each inclination of the head, there is religious significance. The whirling motion induces a trance-like state. The adepts practise the motion from very early youth, which explains their incredible virtuosity, spinning with great speed and ease for long periods of time upon the bare right heel. The group of Dervishes whirl in a great circle – wheels within wheels – perhaps representing the motion of the universe. The origins of whirling are obscure; but apparently the Prophet himself had the habit of leaping up and whirling round when he became excited by an idea.

If it seems odd that such an obviously profound religious ritual should be performed, like a circus act, before crowds of tourists, you should remember that Atatürk banned the Dervish sects altogether. This was a difficult and unpopular move, so it is hardly surprising that the Dervish sects are reviving along with the resurgence of Islam in Turkey. One of the stipulations binding the sects is that their rituals, like the 'Sema', are only to be performed before an audience, thus ensuring that the ritual is no longer an act of serious devotion. The beatific expressions on the faces of the whirling dancers belie this utterly.

If you choose to visit Konya in December to see the 'Sema' make sure you book somewhere to stay well in advance. At this time of year the city is packed solid.

THE LAKES

On the shore of the beautiful BEYŞEHIR GÖLÜ lake, 100 km west of Konya, is BEYŞEHIR. The lake is vast, second in size only to Lake Van, but the water is fresh and teems with fish. It is surrounded by high mountains and is the brightest blue. To the west again, 110 km, looping round the KIZIL DAĞI, you come to EĞRIDIR GÖLÜ, another huge lake, ringed with mountains and full of fish. This lake benefits from the town of EĞRIDIR on its southern shore; it's an attractive town, just starting to make its mark as a tourist destination. It has an incomparable situation, built partly on an island linked to the shore by a causeway. It has good BEACHES, FISHING, RESTAURANTS and HOTELS, and, in the surrounding area, several notable CARA-VANSERAIS.

CAPPADOCIA

Even before man went to the moon, the incredible landscape of the GÖREME region, ancient CAPPADOCIA, was referred to as lunar, since no other adjective could be found; it's quite unlike anywhere else in the world.

The Göreme region lies between the three towns of Kayseri, Aksaray and Niğde and is the geographical centre of the Anatolian plains.

Thousands of years ago, a series of volcanic eruptions from three volcanoes, all now extinct, flooded the Göreme valley with lava. Earthquakes followed, further tormenting the landscape, and over the millennia, the eroding effects of wind and water sculpted the soft volcanic rock into weird and wonderful shapes.

The forests of rock towers, topped with conical 'hats', are amongst the more bizarre sights in a surrealistic landscape of infinite variety. Here, the elements have whittled away the softer, underlying 'tufa', creating towers of soft rock. They are coyly described as FAIRY CHIMNEYS, but look for all the world like a petrified army of giant phalluses.

The 'fairy chimneys' of Cappadocia

The colours of the rock vary enormously, from off-white, through pastel pink and yellow to violet grey, red and brown. To the idiosyncratic artistry of nature, man has added his own dimension. The rock is soft and easy to carve, hardening only after exposure to air. Only rudimentary tools were needed to gouge out, at first, simple caves and then whole communities with kitchens, store-rooms, living quarters and churches.

Still more incredible are the UNDERGROUND CITIES. Owing to their position, plumb in the centre of the Anatolian plain, the Cappadocians were constantly plagued by hostile armies sweeping across their territory. Taking advantage of their unique natural resource, they burrowed into the ground and created huge, subterranean cities in which the population lived, venturing out only to cultivate their fields. One such city was said to be able to accommodate 60,000 people on several different living levels, connected by a labyrinth of tunnels.

There is evidence that the Troglodyte dwellings of Cappadocia were inhabited as far back as 3000 BC, but the area really came into its own when Christian zealots, in search of a hermit lifestyle, found the rock house a perfect, spartan, dwelling place, and the surroundings conducive to solitary contemplation. As Arabs invaded Anatolia in the seventh century, thousands of Christians, fleeing from persecution, descended on Cappadocia, and quite literally went underground in the subterranean cities. Here they stayed, in relative safety, while their would be persecutors thundered by overhead.

When the Arab invasions subsided, the communities moved above ground again, carving churches and monasteries from the tufa and decorating them with elaborate and colourful frescoes.

Christian communities, left to their own devices under the religious tolerance of the Seljuk and Ottoman Empires, continued to inhabit this region until as recently as 50 years ago.

There are still some local people who refuse to budge from their rock dwellings, but most are uninhabited. Some are used as store-houses, as the constant, cool temperature is ideal for preserving fruit and vegetables. The area is surprisingly fertile and Cappadocia is an important agricultural centre and wine-growing region.

The sights worth seeing are spread over a large area and, although exploring on foot is an unbeatable experience, only those with stamina and the luxury of plenty of time could possibly consider this. If you go on an organised tour you will be whisked around all the major sites and put up overnight in one of the big hotels recently built in the area.

But, if you elect to go independently, it's best to try and base yourself in ÜRGÜP, from where you can negotiate a taxi tour of the highlights. Once you've got your bearings, you can explore the more interesting sites at leisure. In some places you can hire a donkey and plod off well away from your fellow tourists to enjoy the scenery.

Ürgüp is a small town and in high season can get very full. There are PANSIYONS and modest HOTELS to be found throughout the area; you shouldn't have trouble finding somewhere to stay unless you are looking for luxury. (All the large hotels get block-booked well in advance by the tour companies, so you will have to book ahead if this is what you want.)

As soon as you arrive in the town you will be approached by all and sundry with offers of taxi tours. Don't agree on anything until you have compared a few prices and you are sure that you will get to see all the main highlights. The Tourist Information Office will help you plan and organise your tour and match you up with other tourists if you are trying to keep the cost down.

Until recently it was impossible to find a decent meal in Ürgüp but the situation has improved considerably, and there are a few RESTAURANTS now serving excellent Turkish food. Look for the ones that are doing brisk business. You may have to wait for a table but you won't go far wrong.

The open air 'MUSEUM' in the valley of Göreme is a must. It is here that you will find the largest concentration of ROCK CHURCHES and MONASTERIES. You can easily spend a whole day here, clambering up to the churches and exploring the pathways and passages in between. The colours of many of the frescoes are still vivid and the scenes they depict quite recognisable.

At ÇAVUŞIN you can see the ruins of the CHURCH OF ST JOHN THE BAPTIST, and in nearby ZELVE stop for a look at more ROCK CHURCHES, a MOSQUE, and the 'Fairy Chimneys' mentioned above. The adventurous and sure-footed can climb up inside some of these rock pillars and look out of the 'windows' carved into the upper levels.

The town of AVANOS is set on the bank of the Kizilırmak, or Red River. One look will tell you how it got its name. The red clay from the river bed is used by local craftsmen for pottery. You can visit their underground workshops and watch them work. You may be asked if you want a go. It's great fun but unless you have some skill, you will splatter yourself and anyone within range, with squelchy red clay, and then feel obliged to buy something, which is the point of the whole exercise. Avanos is also noted for its onyx and alabaster; you could be lucky and find a bargain.

You should find time to see the PERIBACALAR VADISI, the 'Valley of the Fairy Chimneys', and to visit the small town of ORTAHISAR. Here you can climb up inside the huge honeycombed outcrop of rock. At ÜÇHISAR an even more dramatic outcrop offers incredible views of the surrounding valley after a stiff climb to the top.

There are a number of underground cities in the area, but so far only two have been partially excavated and provided with electricity. They are an incredible sight, but a visit to just one is enough to give you a picture of what this subterranean life must have been like. Both at KAYMAKLI and DERINKUYU there are several storeys of living 'cells', meeting rooms, kitchens, churches, store-rooms and cemeteries, connected by a bewildering maze of tunnel passages. Huge round stones were rolled across the entrance to the cities, and at intervals in the internal passageways. The air was kept relatively sweet by central ventilation shafts, although there are no flues for kitchen fires; escaping smoke might have led to discovery. It is believed that there is a passageway connecting Kaymaklı with the city of Derinkuyu some 10 km distant. It has yet to be located, but excavations continue.

Take a sweater when visiting the undergound cities. Whatever the outside temperature, the interior remains constantly cool all year round. Those with dodgy backs beware, for unless you are very short, you are going to spend a great deal of time stooping.

KAYSERI

Formerly Caesarea of the Romans, KAYSERI lies on a high plain at the foot of ERCIYES DAĞI. As another Anatolian capital of the Seljuk Empire, battered and buffeted by Romans, Arabs, Crusaders, Mongols, Tamerlane, Karamans and finally Ottomans, it has a similar history to that of Konya. Today, it is a modest and rather unnattractive city but with some fine Seljuk monuments, tombs and museums. Kayseri is also one of the major centres of the Turkish carpet industry, something you will not be allowed to forget if you visit the town.

Right in the centre of the town is the formidable-looking black CITADEL, built in the sixth century, restored and patched in every subsequent century, and largely surviving today. Next door is the OLD COVERED MARKET; work your way through the various layers of tinkers, tailors, haberdashers, fruiterers and purveyors of meat, vegetables, herbs and spices, until you reach the heart of the BEDESTEN, cobbled and grey, as it was 600 years ago when it was built. Here, under ancient vaults, are stacked fat bales of wool, raw silk from Bursa, soft white cotton, and sacks of downy plastic man-made fibre; bundles of weeds and herbs for dyeing hang in every corner – everything to start your own carpet-making industry. Lurking in every corner, indeed in every corner of the city, are the 'runners' for the carpet-merchants. They are mostly young boys with an astonishing command of English or German, who will engage you easily and disarmingly in conversation, and then lure you to their masters' shops. Here you will be fêted with tea and pleasantries, then pushed and wheedled into buying a carpet, or *Kilim*, or *Cecim*. This is the centre of the industry, and you certainly won't buy cheaper in Istanbul – so if you have a yen to buy a Turkish carpet, this is not a bad place to do it; but be careful, for there are many cheap and wretched imitations.

In the centre of the city, by the Tourist Office, is the ETHNOGRAPHICAL MUSEUM, housed in the HUNAD HATUN MEDRESE. The *medrese* complex itself, with mosque, tomb and religious school, is a fine example of Seljuk architecture; forget the sombre dark stone, and concentrate on the beautiful proportions, design and carving. On exhibition inside the *medrese* is a wonderful collection of Seljuk and Ottoman artefacts: carpets, clothing, pottery, glassware, weapons, coins and tiles; also some fine sculptures and nomadic arts. Apart from Istanbul and Ankara, this is probably one of the better museums in Turkey. In the south-east corner of the *medrese* is the TOMB OF HUNAD HATUN herself, containing her white marble sarcophagus.

'Revolving tomb' — Kayseri

The ULU CAMII, by the market, was originally a thirteenth century Seljuk work, but has had to be rebuilt time after time as it has been so frequently wrecked by earthquakes. The other remaining Seljuk works in the city are tombs, the most interesting of which is the DÖNER KÜMBET, 'Revolving Tomb'.

The tomb doesn't revolve; apparently the idea is that the conical roof is so delicately placed upon the walls, that it could be turned by hand. The tomb is decorated with some fine carvings.

There are two CARAVANSERAIS near Kayseri which are very much worth seeing; in fact, if you see no other caravanserai, make sure you see the SULTAN HAN, for it's the finest Seljuk caravanserai in Turkey, 50 km north-east on the road to SIVAS.

ERCIYES DAĞI is visible from everywhere in the town, its high peaks deep in snow even at the height of summer. If you're tempted by the thought of all that coolness and peace, it's a very easy journey; buses leave for HISARCIK every hour. Hisarcik is a cool retreat from the heat and dust of Kayseri 12 km away in the foothills. From Hisarcik, which has no hotels or restaurants and nothing but tea-houses, it's another 8 km up a cobbled road to the pass at the foot of the mountain. An occasional bus goes this way but you could take a taxi, or hitch – you won't wait more than ten minutes. At the top of the pass are a couple of hotels and a ski-lift; over the road is a lovely spot for camping, a flat green meadow with a stream.

From here it's a fairly steep five hours to the point after which you need ropes, experience and a companion – or eight hours to the summit at 3,871 m.

There are no refuges on the mountain, and no drinking water, so, if you want to make the ascent, leave very early in the morning with plenty of water and food, and good protection against the sun, which is ferocious at this height. You can drive about 2 km past the top ski-lift station, which saves you about 1½ hours walking. It's a rather desolate and barren mountain, but beautiful with spectacular ruddy gold pinnacles and vast fields of grey scree. The lower slopes are alive with flowers, bees and small scuttling creatures; as you climb higher, there are breathtaking views of distant blue mountains, and eagles wheeling below you.

C·H·A·P·T·E·R·8

Inland East

Kars

High on the eastern end of the central Anatolian plateau, at 1,753 m, lies the town of KARS. Today the garrison of Kars protects a major route into Russia, but this has been a strategic outpost on a route well-trodden by traders and conquerors for 2,000 years and more. In the ninth and tenth centuries Kars was the capital of Armenia, the mountainous eastern outpost of Christendom; but as the tides of invasion and conquest swept back and forth through the troubled region, the city was destroyed again and again, until the Russians came at the end of the nineteenth century and laid the foundations for the unprepossessing modern town you see today.

The only monument of any obvious significance is the CITADEL, originally Armenian, but so modified by subsequent incumbents, that little of its original plan is discernible today.

The reason you have come to Kars is to see ANI, a ruined Armenian city, close to the Russian border. The administrative formalities of a visit to Ani can be taken care of by the Tourist Office in Kars, who may also help with the current best way of getting there, for it is 50 km to the east, and there is no regular bus service – try a taxi or *dolmuş*.

Ani has been a settlement of sorts since Urartian times (700 BC), but it was not to reach the peak of its development until it became the capital of the Armenian Bagratid Dynasty, in the tenth century. Then, as capital of the valleys of the Lesser Caucasus Mountains, a wealthy and influential part of Christian Armenia, the city prospered and grew, endowed with many fine churches and monasteries and with a population perhaps as great as 100,000. In 1045 the Byzantines, annexing much of Armenia, conquered the city; 20 years later Alparslan, leading the Seljuk Turks, took it, making it the first Byzantine possession in eastern Anatolia to fall to the Turkish invasion. Then, in the next century, a revival of the vanquished power of Georgia to the east, threw off the Seljuk yoke and liberated a large part of Armenia, including Kars and Ani. Under joint Georgian and Armenian sovereignty, Ani enjoyed a new period of prosperity and stability; but in the fourteenth century, Ghenghis Khan's Mongols stormed out of the east, and another beautiful city was left in bloody ruins. The few inhabitants who had survived the sword, fled to the mountains.

Nobody ever lived at Ani again, save the odd beekeeper or shepherd in his summer tent, and the ruined city, with its glorious Armenian architecture, slumbered for centuries, undisturbed among the weeds. Today it has been 're-discovered' by the hardy few who are prepared to make the journey to eastern Turkey. Although the city lies in ruins, those buildings which have survived represent the finest Armenian architecture in Turkey.

The first sight of the city is the great FORTIFIED WALL, running between the two canyons that form the rest of the city's defences; this was built by the Armenians in the ninth century, though it was later modified by the Seljuks. At the eastern end of the wall is the Georgian CHURCH OF ST GREGORY OF TIGRANE HONENTZ, built in 1215, which contains the best painted and carved frescoes in the city; these are typical of the wonderful representations of saints and animals which feature so much in Georgian and Armenian decorative art.

After the conquest, the Seljuks built the MOSQUE OF MENUCHER, which shows clearly how much they were influenced by the Armenian style. This is the only surviving mosque, although the beautiful CATHEDRAL in the centre of the old city did a stretch as a mosque after the Seljuk conquest; later the Georgians restored it, and what you see today is the remains of the very pinnacle of Armenian art.

The valleys and hills that surround Ani and Kars are rich in ruined monasteries and churches, both Armenian and Georgian. The military restrictions make it difficult to visit them, but, for the curious and bold, there is always a way. The MONASTERY OF ST JOHN is 15 km north-east of Ani; BAGNAIR MONASTERY 20 km west, near Kozluca. MAGAZBERT KALESI is 2 hours walk south-west on the Arpaçay river.

DOĞUBEYAZIT

Unfortunately there is no direct route from Kars to Doğubeyazıt; if there were, it would run through eastern Turkey's most spectacular mountains, finally skirting Mount Ararat itself. You must take a bus via Horasan, which makes it about an eight hour ride.

Carving of 'Tree of Life' from Işak Paşa Sarayı

Doğubeyazıt is famous for the IŞAK PAŞA SARAYI, which you may have seen on the cover of many of the brochures enticing you to come to Turkey. An arrival by night is recommended; put up at the ISFAHAN HOTEL, the only 'fancy' hotel in a very sleepy town. The thing to do is to get up just before dawn and look north for your first view of AĞRI DAĞI – Mount Ararat. Whether you love or loathe mountains, this one will take your breath away; its great feature is that, like Mount Fuji in Japan, it is perfectly mountain-shaped, like a picture-book mountain, and it so dwarfs the surrounding hills, that it seems to rise sheer from the plain to its peak, shrouded in eternal snows at 5,182 m. No wonder it abounds in such legends. To see the first rays of the sun as they strike the snow of the peak is a glorious sight; all through the day the light plays tricks with the mountain, so that it appears to change altogether, every three or four minutes; sometimes it appears as a hill just outside the town, then it may fill the whole sky, and in another moment, be quite invisible. When you've feasted your eyes on Ararat, scan the rest of the horizon, for Doğubeyazıt is surrounded by the most curiously shaped hills, the twisted remains of some antediluvian cataclysm; blue and pink and orange in the first light of day, they take on the eerie semblance of a Martian landscape. Now you can go back to bed, but not for too long, for the next recommendation is an early morning walk up to the Işak Paşa Sarayı.

Follow the high street to the east, cross the roundabout by the statue of Atatürk, and keep going straight up the hill for an hour and a half; this may seem excessive, but it's worth it. Later in the day there are any number of taxis, *dolmuşes* or tour buses climbing to the palace, but nothing compares with spotting the dramatic blue silhouette, dim in a distant cleft of the hills, and watching it slowly loom nearer with the sun rising behind the jagged mountains that surround it.

The palace opens at eight, and if you can contrive to get there by then, you should have it all to yourself. There is great diversity of opinion as to its founder and its age – differing accounts vary by as much as 1,000 years.

It is generally thought that the fortified palace was built round about the end of the eighteenth century, by Işak Paşa, a powerful and wealthy warlord who had the responsibility of guarding the pass through to Persia. The palace he built, which is the very stuff of the legendary 'oriental pleasure-dome', is a spectacularly eccentric mixture of styles – Armenian, Georgian, Seljuk and Persian; the Armenian and Georgian in the exuberant stone-carved lions, flowers and trees; the Seljuk in the richly decorated portals; and the Persian in the brick striped minaret. The mosque beneath its deep dome is plain and unadorned; the harem, courts, reception halls and other grand rooms are decorated with spectacular stone-carving, but the barracks, granaries, guardrooms and other more mundane quarters are mostly destroyed. The safety of walking beneath some of the teetering blocks of masonry is questionable, but the palace, with its stupendous setting is a truly exciting historical monument; it's a pity its origins and history are not better documented.

It is said to be possible to obtain permission to climb Mount Ararat; with one foot in Iran, one in Russia and one in Turkey, it is understandably a sensitive military zone. In reality, if you contact the authorities, or the Turkish Mountaineering Club in Ankara, you will get no help and a great deal of obstruction. (I do not know of anybody who has received permission to climb it, apart from the swarms of American Christian Fundamentalist groups squabbling over bits of wood, purported to be from Noah's Ark.) The foothills can be reached from Doğubeyazıt, Iğdir or from Aralık. Guides and muleteers will offer their services from all these places.

Van

Continuing down the eastern border of Turkey, the next town worth stopping at is VAN, a modern town, swarming with Kurds, Iranians, Turks and tourists. Here are good HOTELS with up-market RESTAURANTS; the nicest place to eat in the evenings is the KÖŞK, where you eat outside in the garden; an atmosphere of gastronomic abandon prevails among the locals who patronise the place – the food is good and the prices reasonable. Van is also an important trading centre; here you can buy coarse, gaily-coloured Kurdish carpets and rugs, and much finer work, imported from Tabriz, across the Iranian border. You pay less if you buy here than you would in Istanbul, but you still have to fight hard to get a bargain. The museum too, is worth a look, for everything you don't see in the various archaeological sites around the town is here: Urartian artefacts, the ubiquitous Hittite lions lurking in the garden, and a fine exhibition of nineteenth-century Ottoman clothing, jewellery, pistols and daggers, etc. Don't overlook the astonishing VAN CAT; these long-haired white cats are peculiar in that they have one blue eye and one yellow one – this is not a ploy of the Tourist Authority to persuade you to visit Van, it is true.

The celebrated ROCK OF VAN is 3 km west of the town centre, set on the edge of the lake. This citadel rock and the

Seljuk türbe and mosque near Van

ruins that lie beneath it, are all that remains of the ancient city of
Van. Originally founded by the Urartians perhaps in 1000 BC, it
has survived conquest variously by the Medes, the Persians in
the fifth century, the Armenians, Seljuks and even the Mongols
until, in 1387, Tamerlane decided to do the job properly and
destroyed the lot. What remained of the town eventually
became part of the Ottoman Empire in 1534, but it continued to
decline until the First World War, when it was thoroughly
sacked by the Russians. Today it is a spectacular ruin with faint
traces of everybody who held sway here. Visit the site in the
evening, when it's cool and, from the citadel, you can watch the
sun set over Lake Van and the ruins of the city below.

One's impression of a place depends largely upon how one
arrives; the best way to arrive at Van is at dawn or sunset, having
crossed the great lake by steamer. LAKE VAN is a vast inland
sea, a glorious expanse of blue water ringed by high
mountains, set at 1,677 m on the central Anatolian plateau. It
has a very high mineral and saline content which makes it
disagreeable for fish, and few can survive in it; but it's pleasant
to swim in, cool in the hot summer, with a strange soft oily
sensation – but try and keep it out of your mouth, it tastes awful!
There are good beaches south-west of Van, as far as GEVAŞ.
The steamer does the crossing from TATVAN to Van in four
hours; but unfortunately the times of sailing are completely
unpredictable – even the Tourist Information Offices don't
know them. It's said to depend upon the arrival of a given
quantity of vegetables which makes up most of the boat's load.
The only thing to do is to wait on the dock (*Iskele*) at Van or
Tatvan until the boat goes; sometimes there are two a day,

sometimes only one. It's no luxury cruise, and there's little in the way of food; but it can be a wonderful experience, sailing high among these savage, barren mountains.

It is also advisable to avoid staying in Tatvan at the western end of the lake, as the hotel accommodation is grim, and the town dismal. If you are unfortunate enough to be stranded here, however, you can mitigate your melancholy by making an expedition to NEMRUT DAĞI (not to be confused with the big one further west). This one is an extinct volcano, 3,048 m high; a stiff four-hour climb starting from north-east of the town, or a 30 km taxi-ride to the top. The crater is one of the largest in the world, almost 7 km in diameter; it contains a beautiful crescent lake, set in fantastic contortions of solidified lava. You can clamber 500 m down from the rim to the lake below.

Some 40 km south-west of Van, on the road that skirts the southern shore of the lake, you come to the *Iskele* (jetty) for AKDHAMAR ISLAND; by the road is a tolerable LOKANTA where you can wait for the arrival of enough tourists to fill a boat out to the island – you won't wait long, for there are several boats and plenty of tourists to fill them. On the island is the tenth century Armenian CHURCH OF THE HOLY CROSS and the ruins of a MONASTERY. The church, set on a little hill in a grove of olives and pines, is very well preserved; it is said to be one of the best surviving examples of Armenian architecture in Turkey. The carved stone friezes around the top are almost intact and you can still make out the various stories depicted – Jonah and the Whale (a rather jolly creature with a big grin), Abraham and Isaac, George and the Dragon; as well as these there are lions, dragons, rams, goats, deer and a whole host of saints, all intertwined with grape-laden vines. Inside the church, the painting, with which the whole church would have been adorned, has nearly all worn away but the architecture remains, with its high central dome, tiled on the outside and the tall vaults, supported on simple pillars. Here are all the finest elements of Armenian religious building and design.

It has always been considered strange that Tamerlane, having polished off the Rock of Van, didn't turn his attentions to the destruction of this Christian church. The only explanation offered is that the sanctuary was saved by its fine hunting reliefs – hunting having been second only to slaughter and pillage as Tamerlane's favourite pastimes.

In the eleventh century, the island was an important centre of the Kingdom of Armenia. On the hill at the western end of the island, King Gagik built a royal palace; unfortunately, not a stone remains today.

When you've had enough of the pleasures of history and fine and graceful architecture, dive off the rocks into the cool clear water, or clamber down to the shingle BEACH on the south side below the church.

On the road to HAKKARI, 45 km south-east of Van, is the slatternly village of GÜZELSU; on a crag dominating the town is the black CASTLE OF HOŞAP. The castle crawls up the rock, its thick walls of coarse black stone, half hewn from the rock itself. Most of the castle is in ruins, but the outer walls, with their turrets and towers, survive, as does the gloomy main gate with its cylindrical towers.

The Mahmoudis, a Turkic tribe under the protection of the Ottomans, built this castle in 1643. From the top turret you can look out over the awful barren hills of the Mahmoudis' kingdom, and you might wonder why on earth anyone would want to rule such a land; the Güzelsu (Beautiful Water) creates a ribbon of green, but the hills are cracked and waterless.

Between Hoşap and Van, you pass the ridge of ÇAVUŞTEPE. Straddling the ridge are the remains of an URARTIAN CITY. There's little left to thrill anyone but an archaeologist, but the site is impressive, as always – crowning a ridge overlooking a rich agricultural valley that is as flat as a billiard-table. The huge stone blocks, perfectly interlocking, and the firm straight lines of the streets and walls give a good idea of the solidity and strength that must have been the hallmark of Urartian cities.

The Tourist Office in Van will arrange mini-buses to take you to all the surrounding sites in one day – this is worth doing; if you would care to linger, go back the next day.

If you continue along the road to HAKKARI, after much tortuous climbing and descending, you arrive at YÜKSEKOVA. Here, in the SAT and CILO Mountains, are some of the wildest and most unexplored parts of Turkey; high peaks and glaciers up to 4,115 m and, below, deep, glaciated valleys, teeming with game and carpeted with wild flowers. These are peaks for serious mountaineers.

This is the heart of ancient Kurdistan, the mountainous land of the Kurds, which, straddling the borders of Iraq, Iran and Turkey, has been fiercely disputed for centuries and remains so to this day. This part of Turkey, around Lake Van, is still heavily populated by the Kurds, a fiercely independent people, chafing under the Turkish yoke. The Turks refuse to recognise them as an independent people, referring to them as 'Mountain Turks'; the Kurds, in return, despise the Turks, and are still given to banditry and rebellion whenever the opportunity presents itself.

Dıyarbakır

The road from Tatvan down off the high plateau to DIYARBAKIR enters the GÜZELDERE, or beautiful valley, just before BITLIS – a sad grey town, clinging to the sides of the gorge like a slug on a flowerpot. For mile after mile the road descends in the bed of the gorge, sometimes through steep mountains, forested and green, sometimes through dry, black crags and sometimes through baking hills of sand. Eventually, having passed through every imaginable type of landscape, you burst into the terrible plains around Diyarbakır. For hours you drive on across the plain, then down across the TIGRIS and up to the black city walls of Diyarbakır, roasting in a hollow.

In summer, the air of Diyarbakır is like a blast from an oven; the city is known as the hottest in Turkey. As the result of a long period of Arab domination, the town-centre today, almost unchanged for 200 years, has a marked Arabic flavour, an exotic and rather wild atmosphere. For those who find the western towns of Turkey excessively European, Diyarbakır is the antidote.

The most striking historical remains in the city are the old black WALLS, the oldest and finest in Anatolia, with their MONUMENTAL GATES, and the ULU CAMII, the Great Mosque. This mosque, the very first of the Seljuk Great Mosques of Anatolia built in 1091, is much more typical of Arab architecture than the other mosques of Turkey; it has an unusual square minaret, surmounting a great colonnaded courtyard with two interesting şadırvans (drinking and washing fountains), the whole thing made of the local dark grey basalt. A constant bustle of commercial and religious activity swells around the courts and portals, spilling over from the surrounding market streets; a warren of narrow cobbled alleys with canvas awnings for shade, and every conceivable type of workshop and emporium.

Deep in this labyrinth is a hidden and locked BYZANTINE CHURCH, once half-heartedly converted to a mosque, but now long disused. An old woman is the unofficial caretaker, and, if you make yourself conspicuous, she will unlock the door for you.

Crossing the main street to the south of the Ulu Camii, you come to a fine old COVERED MARKET, now used as a meat and offal market. One of the great pleasures of Diyarbakır is that nothing has been polished and sanitised for the tourist; the whole city is a living historical monument.

There are also two fine sixteenth-century OTTOMAN CARA-VANSERAIS, one, the DELILLER HANI is near the MARDIN

KAPISI (gate); the other, the HASAN PAŞA HANI, is near the central intersection of the four main city roads. The way to enjoy Diyarbakır is to expect to be roasted alive, and to lose oneself wandering in the convoluted streets of the old town. It is a staunchly conservative Islamic city; the sort of place where it's better not to wear shorts.

There is a reasonable HOTEL midway between the *Otogar* and the city-centre, with probably the best restaurant in town. Be careful what you eat, for the heat here makes food go bad very quickly.

Leaving Diyarbakır towards the west, you pass through some unimaginably barren landscapes; stark plains littered with hot black stones and tufts of dry grass. Black Tent Nomads live here, for, incredibly enough, these plains grow barley and are grazed by sheep and cattle. Three hours of this and you cross the swift green EUPHRATES, known in antiquity as the River of Desire, a magnificent river watering a wide, fertile valley.

There is a plan, currently being initiated, to dam the Euphrates and irrigate the 'Land Between the Rivers', to create a new fertile Mesopotamia. Understandably, there is intense opposition from environmentalists, who are concerned about the long-term effects of such a drastic change upon the climate, flora and fauna; and from historians and archaeologists who see one of the 'Cradles of Civilisation' about to be flooded. On the other hand, if the plan comes to fruition, it will bring prosperity and employment to a poor and depressed part of Turkey.

Beyond the Euphrates, the plain puckers into a glorious contortion of coloured hills, footing the mountains where NEMRUT DAĞI rises.

Nemrut Daği

There are two ways to get to Mount Nemrut, yet another highlight of Turkish tourist literature. The more direct route is from MALATYA, where a good road has recently been pushed through to the mountain. Malatya Tourist Office can help you join a mini-bus excursion; this should, hopefully, replace the wretched route from KAHTA.

Kahta is a town which has little to recommend it. As you arrive, you will be set upon by flocks of touts, gabbling at you in an extraordinary language composed of various elements of Turkish, German, American serviceman's slang and Pidgin French, and understandable to nobody. Each will badger you to take advantage of his particular offer of hotels, taxis and mini-bus tours.

The standard procedure is to take a mini-bus to the top of Mount Nemrut, leaving in summer at 2.00 a.m. in order to arrive at the summit as the sun is rising. In practice the buses do not leave until there are enough tourists to fill them, and when they do go, they drive dangerously on treacherous mountain roads. In recent years there was an accident in which a mini-bus with a tired driver rolled off the road and down the mountain; the driver was killed and several tourists were badly injured; the local *Jandarma* (army) would do nothing to help, neither did any of the passers-by, with one or two sterling exceptions.

The peak of Mount Nemrut is about 70 km from Kahta, and takes 2½ to 3 hours to reach on an extremely tortuous road; on the way, you pass a spectacular ROMAN BRIDGE, crossing the RIVER CENDERE where it emerges from a gorge into a broad valley. Here, as at every village and stopping-place along the road, ragged flocks of children will descend upon you, and if you fail to grant their demands of cigarettes and money, will beat your car with sticks and throw stones at you.

(The reader may have noticed a lack of enthusiasm for this area, and put it down to a simple bad experience – for inevitably one's views about a place are coloured by the pleasures or miseries experienced there.)

The actual mountain site is stupendous, if only as a monument to the vanity and folly of man. In a way you feel that you shouldn't go and see it, in order not to indulge the megalomania of the man who had it built. In the first century BC, Mithridates, King of the Commagenes, the barren mountain kingdom that you look upon from the summit, decided to build a mausoleum for his royal line and himself. So great was the importance that this man attached to himself in the great scheme of things, that he deemed it fitting that he and his ancestors should be depicted in colossal form, sitting with the gods themselves. To this end, an army of tens of thousands must have toiled for years to build his colossal monument to vanity, the only achievement for which king and kingdom are known.

Nemrut is the highest mountain in the range, and can be seen from a distance as a perfect pyramid with a yellowish pimple for a peak. The pimple is a shaly pyramid, 90 m high, and from the top there is a tremendous view of the mountains you've just passed through. On the east and west sides are terraces where the fabulous heads of Mithridates, his father Antiochus, various gods and a number of lions and eagles, stare phlegmatically into the distance – or lie with their noses in the dust, where earthquakes have toppled them. The stone-carving and design is, in fact, very fine indeed. It is said that the best time to view

The monument of the Commagene Kings on Mount Nemrut

the site is at sunrise, and the light is glorious then. Unfortunately, the recommendation hasn't been lost on other visitors, and there are so many other tourists that the mystery and beauty of the scene are lost, the silence flawed by the clatter of camera-shutters.

There is one *dolmuş* a day from Kahta to ESKI KAHTA, at the foot of the mountain; it leaves at 3.00 p.m. from the mini-bus station 500 m down the road from the *Otogar*. In Eski Kahta there are small GUEST-HOUSES and you can hire mules and guides for the five hour climb to the summit. If you're not accustomed to it, ten hours on a mule is not a pleasant experience.

C·H·A·P·T·E·R· 9

The Black Sea Coast

In every way the BLACK SEA COAST is quite different from the rest of Turkey; the land is lush and green, even in the middle of summer. This is due to the fairly reliable summer rains, coaxed from the moist air of the Black Sea by the chain of mountains that runs the length of the coast. In summer the weather is hot, though not with the fearful unrelenting heat of central Anatolia or the south coast; but hot enough to make the cool water of the Black Sea a blessed relief. It may rain as much as once a week in summer, just enough to lay the dust and draw the scents of the plants and flowers that grow in such wild profusion. The winters are mild with regular snow, sometimes as much as 1 m deep on the coast itself.

There are few Classical remains on this shore; the Greeks and other Mediterranean peoples who built cities on Turkey's other coasts, found this area uncongenial, and, though there were important settlements here, much of what they did build has long since been destroyed or washed away. That is not to say that there is nothing to see, for what remains of the Byzantine and Ottoman presence makes a fascinating counterpoint to the glories of the natural scenery.

If you have only visited Istanbul and the popular tourist resorts of south and west Anatolia, you will soon realise that in terms of investment and development, the Black Sea coast is a backwater. The local people are very keen – almost desperate – that the tourist boom which has enriched the southern coasts of Turkey, should also find its way up here and give them a fair slice of the cake. The government, though sharing this view, is not forthcoming with the funds, so the local people scrimp and save to fund their own development. The result is enormous enthusiasm, but less finesse. There are very few luxurious hotels and facilities for the tourist, but what hotels, restaurants, tea-gardens and guided tours there are, make up for their slender means with friendliness and eagerness to please.

The result is that there are very few foreign tourists; so if you decide to visit the Black Sea coast, you will find it quiet and largely unspoilt, the people curious, friendly and hospitable, and prices rock-bottom; pretty good reasons for a visit.

WEST OF SAMSUN

From ŞILE, 80 km north-east of Istanbul, a road runs along the coast as far as the Russian border at Hopa, over 1,000 km away. Şile is a popular resort for Istanbulus, who come to bathe from the town's fine sandy BEACHES in one of the safer areas of the Black Sea. (Many Black Sea beaches are cursed with a strong undertow, which can make bathing hazardous; you are generally safe in a sheltered bay, where there is a shallow sloping shelf of sand, or preferably where there are others swimming.) The beaches are good too, at AKÇAKOCA, 180 km to the east. Both towns are well supplied with modest ACCOMMODATION and RESTAURANTS, but apart from the beaches, and the ruined GENOESE CASTLES that stand above each town, there is nothing really spectacular.

ZONGULDAK is the major city of this part of the coast; an important coal-mining and industrial centre, it sprawls, huge and sooty across the coastal plain to the busy artificial harbour. This is no place for the visitor in search of pleasure, but high in the mountains behind the city is the lovely YEDIGÖLLER NATIONAL PARK, one of Turkey's most popular mountain resorts, an unspoilt wilderness of deciduous forests with swift mountain rivers and clear lakes. BOLU and SAFRANBOLU (famous for their fine old wooden Ottoman houses) are the towns to make for.

East of Zonguldak there are several small towns with good beaches – ABANA and INEBOLU – but the interesting part of the coast does not begin until SINOP; in fact, if you want to explore the Black Sea coast, the best way is to take a bus direct to Sinop, about twelve hours from Istanbul.

Sinop

A market town and fishery for the small agricultural area in the foothills of the ISFENDIYAR MOUNTAINS, SINOP first appears in the eighth century BC, as a colony of the Miletians. It became an important port under the Romans, and later it was the main Black Sea base of the Ottoman fleet. Recently it has declined in importance, mainly as a result of the difficulty of access; the road running along this part of the Black Sea coast has only recently been constructed. Previously, the only land communication had been directly over a formidable mountain pass.

The OLD TOWN, with its fine natural harbour, is built on a peninsula in the shadow of an extinct volcano. The remains of a magnificent BYZANTINE CITADEL now house the bus-station; clamber through the mulberry trees and out onto the battlements for a bird's eye view of the town and wonderful views of the mighty stone walls, sheering straight down into the sea.

Down the hill in the town, there's a fishing harbour with a promenade, RESTAURANTS with vine-shaded terraces, and a couple of good waterfront HOTELS. Here you can hire a boat and tackle, for a day's FISHING in the Black Sea, or take a *Kayık* to one of the many BEACHES near the town. The back streets are full of delightful wooden OTTOMAN HOUSES, mostly in an advanced state of decay; contented Turkish dogs and chickens monopolise the shade of overhanging eaves and fig-trees. The ALAEDDIN CAMII, in the centre of town, is a good example of a late Seljuk mosque, with its fine relief-work framing the door, and spectacularly carved *minber*.

Gerze

A 40 minute bus-ride to the east is GERZE, a tiny fishing town at the foot of the KÜRE MOUNTAINS, which unaccountably has a direct bus-link to Istanbul and Ankara. The setting is incomparable, among small farms, in well wooded country with the blue mountains soaring behind. But the town itself is poor, and despite its tea-gardens by the jetty and its fishing boats, not very picturesque. Come here for the beautiful countryside, quiet unspoilt BEACHES and clear sea. The town HOTEL is modest.

Heading east again, the road winds along the gentle slopes of the mountains, just above the shore; below, through the fields and woods, are quiet coves and beaches, with perhaps the lone house of a fisherman, farmer or boat-builder – lovely country for CAMPING.

Then, 80 km east, you come to BAFRA, on the delta of the KIZILIRMAK, one of the great rivers of Anatolia. As with most river deltas, this one is fertile, flat, sandy and dull. Further east is the almost identical delta of the YEŞILIRMAK. Between the two deltas lies SAMSUN, the major industrial city of this coast, famous mostly for its tobacco, its busy port and its historical connections with Atatürk's founding of the republic. It was here that he disembarked in May 1919 and played the first stroke that would unite the army and the Turkish people to fight for the tattered remnants of their country. There is a wonderful STATUE of Atatürk on horseback, but that hardly makes ugly, industrial Samsun a place worth visiting. Should you find yourself stranded here for some reason, the best thing to do would be to take a bus or a slow train up over the mountains to AMASYA.

Nineteenth-century Ottoman houses

Amasya is built in a deep valley of the Yeşilırmak, and its beautiful wooden houses, lining the riverbank, are a popular theme of Turkish tourist posters. Apart from this, the town was used as a testing-ground for apprentice Ottoman sultans, who would be sent here to govern the province for a few years before they took the real reins of power in Istanbul; as a result, the town is richly endowed with fine MOSQUES and TOMBS.

EAST OF SAMSUN

Some 90 km east of SAMSUN lies what is described as 'The Pearl of the Black Sea Coast', ÜNYE. The town itself is not particularly beautiful, and the setting isn't enhanced by the busy road thundering between the town and the beach promenade, a problem Ünye has in common with all Black Sea resorts; often there is simply nowhere else to put the road. But the bay, with its shelving sandy BEACHES, is beautiful. To the east, cape after cape recedes into the distant blue, scarcely discernible from the sea and sky. Here you will find safe, sandy beaches, camp-sites and seaside pinewoods; there is a good tourist HOTEL in the town too, the Kumsal, whose RESTAU-RANT is Ünye's best.

East of Ünye, on the way to ORDU, lies the most beautiful part of the Black Sea coast, the YASON PROMONTORY, named after Jason the Argonaut. Here the mountains are steeper and lush, with deep green groves of hazelnut, plunging almost vertically to the sea. The road runs along a winding CORNICHE with dramatic views of the sea battering the black rocks below, or rolling up the beaches into the coves.

BOLAMAN is a pretty little village with decaying wooden *Yalıs* (seaside villas), a fishing harbour, a LOKANTA and a tiny BEACH. All around the cape the villages are utterly unspoilt and mostly too small to warrant a name. The ground is fertile, with rich crops of vegetables, fruit and nuts; there is spring-water from the mountains, and the fish are fresh from the sea. There are no hotels, no tourists, just beautiful scenery, friendly people and clean sea for swimming.

Behind the cape are MOUNTAIN VILLAGES, connected by rough dirt-roads that wind through the river valleys, and endless miles of tortuous, cobbled footpaths. The villages themselves have changed little, either architecturally or in lifestyle, since the days of the Kingdom of Pontica, 1,000 years ago. Walking along the cobbled tracks through tunnels of rich greenery, you will see more flowers and butterflies than you ever dreamed of. In the steep fields and woods around the villages are sheep, goats, bees, fruit and *fındık* (hazelnuts), for this region is the world's greatest cultivator of hazelnuts, producing some 300,000 tonnes a year.

The main town on the cape is PERŞEMBE, with good BEACHES, RESTAURANTS, seafront TEA-GARDENS and a good modern tourist HOTEL, the VONA, which has the town's best restaurant.

ORDU, the next town, has miles of beaches, good hotels, restaurants and CAMPSITES.

A BYZANTINE FORTRESS crowns the great rock around which lies the town of GIRESUN. The view from the top of the hill gives a clear idea of what can be done by town-planners and developers to ruin a beautiful site; for Giresun, which seems charmless from within, reveals itself from above, as beyond redemption. Clustered on the north side of the rock, is the OLD TOWN, now a run-down, but beautiful residential quarter. On every corner of the narrow, cobbled streets are Byzantine pillars, arches and doorways, incorporated into the gardens and walls of later Ottoman town-houses; these too are on their last legs, teetering precariously, their elegance now faded and patched, cracked by neglect and the roots of fig-trees.

Heading east from Giresun, the coast is again steep, rocky and unspoilt, with good bathing from rocks and beaches all the way. TIREBOLU is an interesting little town; 100 years ago it must have been beautiful, with its fine situation on three little headlands with a fishing harbour, a BYZANTINE FORTRESS and the steep hills behind. It is still attractive today, with its square houses with elaborately carved wooden balconies and kiosk-like windows, but unfortunately, poverty has resulted in extreme decay, and the once proud little town is now cracked and crumbling. RESTAURANTS are few and limited, and HOTELS are clean, but extremely modest. The locals yearn for the golden touch of tourism, but for the moment it just passes them by.

TRABZON

Tourism has discovered TRABZON, and with good reason, for although the town no longer has the romantic associations of Rose McCaulay's *Towers of Trebizond*, the city has a rich historical heritage, and is set in some of northern Turkey's most spectacular scenery.

The town and port were founded in the eighth century BC, by the merchants of Sinope; it was well placed for trade from the East, whence came caravans laden with exotic goods from Persia and China. The Romans developed this trade and, under the Emperor Hadrian, Trapezus, as it was then known, became ·an important city, the capital of the Kingdom of Pontica.

When Constantinople was sacked by the Crusaders in 1204, the Emperor Alexis Comnenus fled to Trebizond. There he set up an independent kingdom, maintaining a precarious peace through treaties with the surrounding Turkish tribes. The city prospered and grew fat, for long continuing to survive as an island of Old Byzantium in a sea of Turks; it is from this time that the best monuments survive.

But by 1461, Mehmet the Conqueror, who now ruled the burgeoning Ottoman Empire from Istanbul, decided to bring the Christian kingdom of Pontica under the Ottoman yoke. After a gruelling march through the high passes of the Pontic Alps, he appeared before the great walls of the city with an army that was hopelessly ill-equipped to deal with such fortifications. (This was out of character for Mehmet, who had already shown himself to be one of the most provident and efficient conquerors in history.) King David Comnenus however, in return for safe conduct and leniency, handed over the keys without a shot being fired. Almost the entire population was enslaved, and thousands re-located to populate the 'Great City', Istanbul.

Under the Ottomans the city continued in importance, becoming by the mid-nineteenth century, the world centre for trade in leeches, arsenic, opium and rhubarb. In 1917 the Russians moved in and used the city as the headquarters for their short-lived invasion of north-eastern Turkey.

Today, Trabzon has a thriving industrial area and an important Black Sea harbour, but the centre of town has much to offer the tourist. The black CITY WALLS on the hill to the west of the modern city-centre, mark the extent of the ancient city; here are the oldest mosques; the severe, unornamented ORTAHISAR CAMII – converted after 1461 from the Comnene's church of Panaghia Chrysokephalos; and the fine ŞIRIN HATUN CAMII. In the northern corner of the citadel is the old ÇIFTE HAMAM, the 'Double Bath', which, along with the SEKIZ DIREK HAMAM, two blocks north-west, is as old and as elegant as you will find anywhere in this part of Turkey.

A couple of blocks north-east of the Citadel is the BAZAAR area, with its old covered market and *Hans;* this is the most interesting part of the city, combining the timeless fascination of an Asian market with some of the city's best mosques, baths and *Hans.*

The MEYDAN or Main Square, is the centre of modern Trabzon; here are the TOURIST OFFICE, main BANKS, city bus-station and a tree-shaded park. Just east of this square, past the ISKENDER PAŞA CAMII, are the best HOTELS and most of the best RESTAURANTS in town. On the east side of ISKELE

CADDESI, leading from the square down to the sea, there is a good ROOFTOP RESTAURANT that catches sea and mountain breezes and serves some of the best food in Trabzon. At the foot of Iskele Caddesi and 200 m east along the front, is a shady TEA-GARDEN, perched on a rock over the sea.

From the centre, 2 km west, is the late BYZANTINE CHURCH of AGHIA SOFIA, built in 1245. It is a pleasingly simple building in the shape of a Greek Cross, with a high dome supported by four marble pillars. The beautiful frescoes which survive – the best of which are in the dome and narthex – are said to be some of the very finest examples of Byzantine art. The situation itself is delightful. The church is set in an unkempt little garden, full of tall grass and wild flowers, on a hillock overlooking the sea.

Trabzon's other attraction is the ATATÜRK SUMMERHOUSE, built with a subscription raised by the citizens. It is a simple villa in white wood and marble, standing in a garden on a hill overlooking the city. The rooms are stuffed with Atatürk memorabilia – books, maps, photographs, etc. – and simply furnished with the furniture and carpets used by the great man himself.

There is an airport with daily flights from Istanbul and Ankara, but an increasingly popular way of reaching Trabzon is to take the weekly STEAMER from Istanbul; it leaves Istanbul on a Thursday morning, and arrives on Saturday afternoon. Buy your ticket from the Turkish Maritime Agency, the big building housing the Liman Restaurant by the Galata bridge, in Karaköy, Istanbul.

SUMELA

The SUMELA MONASTERY, or Meryemana as the Turks call it, is surely one of the most magnificent sights in Turkey. Outside the Trabzon Tourist Office, a line of *dolmuşes* waits to take groups of four or five tourists for the 1¼ hour drive 60 km to the monastery. You head out of town on the mountain road to Erzurum; at the market town of MAÇKA, turn left and continue up a steep narrowing valley with a rushing river and soaring pine-clad hills. This is a National Park and a good introduction to the beauty of these, the 'Pontic Alps' behind Trabzon. The car park is in a grassy meadow by a waterfall, looking for all the world like the Turkish vision of Paradise you see painted on the sides of lorries; a wooden bridge crosses the river by a restaurant where you buy meat by the kilo and barbecue it outside by your table; drinks come from the icy clear water of the river.

As you stand at the foot of the great cliff, you catch a glimpse of the monastery through the pines, and you can hardly believe your eyes; it is like a vast eagle's eyrie, clinging to a sheer wall of rock. Through the woods a steep path winds up and up – about 20 minutes stiff climb.

The core of the monastery is a little church, built in the fourth century by Greek monks; you can still see the remains of the church, tiny, crudely constructed of coarse stone, but in itself a remarkable feat of engineering . Around the church there grew a huge monastery which reached its zenith in the fourteenth century as an important theological school; it contained a noted library and a number of sacred treasures, including an icon attributed to St Luke. It continued to function as a monastery until the expulsion of the Greeks in 1923.

Much of the monastery is in ruins now, but you can still see the basic outline, and many of the richly coloured frescoes have survived, although they are too badly defaced to be easily recognised.

EAST OF TRABZON

Heading east again from Trabzon you follow the coast, as always, passing through villages and small towns with fishing harbours, beaches and seaside *lokantas*. The landscape behind the shore becomes even more dramatic; the hills, now cloaked with tea-plantations instead of hazelnut, are almost vertical. The hills and rocks are a riot of vegetation, and the colour of the tea-fields is the deepest green you'll ever see, dotted with women tea-pickers in gaily-coloured scarves and aprons, like butterflies in a meadow. This part of the country is notorious for the custom of sending the women to work in the fields, while the men idle the day away in the tea-house.

Soon you reach OF, the town where you turn for the high pass to Bayburt. Whichever route you take from Trabzon to the interior, you are bound to cross some spectacular mountain pass; the main road to Erzurum snakes up the dramatic Zigana Pass to Gümüşhane at 2,011 m; but the Çaykara pass on the road between Of and Bayburt is the highest and wildest in Turkey, at 2,286 m. It is traversed by enthusiastic mini-buses, bursting with passengers, all of whom seem quite unconcerned by the narrow escapes from death occasioned by every bend. The steep slopes of the mountains on the north side are well populated – houses and farms appear in the most astonishing places; breathtaking vistas of deep gorges, waterfalls and high, flower-spangled meadows, change with every turn. At the top, above the tree-line, there are high mountain grazing lands, with patches of summer snow. This journey is not for the faint-hearted; the road is rough and narrow, and there are no protective parapets, so, if a vehicle comes tearing round a corner in the opposite direction, as they so frequently do, it is only the will of Allah that keeps you from the abyss.

Descending to the other side, you would think you were in a different world, for after the deluges on the steep northern slopes, there is no rain left to water the dusty hills of the southern side. Here, you have left verdant Europe, for the harsh steppes of Asia.

A long, steady descent takes you to BAYBURT, a market town on the main Trabzon-Erzurum road. Once, along with KALE to the west, the southern defensive line of the Kingdom of Pontica, the town lies in a dramatic setting beneath a cliff capped with a great fortress. This castle was originally built before the age of Byzantium, but has been extensively patched up through the ages. Now you can clamber up on the well-preserved walls and admire the town below, with its torrent of a river cutting it in two; or gaze at the beautiful Pontic Mountains to the north. The castle of Kale is even more formidable.

Back on the north coast, the next town you come to is RIZE. Rize is where 90 per cent of Turkish tea comes from – 569,000 tonnes of it a year. As a result, the town is a little more prosperous than other Black Sea towns, with fine modern buildings and opulent seaside villas. The town itself revolves almost entirely round the tea trade, apart from which it is not especially interesting. The best visit is the INSTITUTE OF TEA with its pretty tea-garden, set on a hill with a lovely view of the bay, and a less lovely view of the town below.

The next town, Ardeşen, is only 60 km from the Russian border; from here another road leads into the mountains, to ÇAMLIHEMSIN. Mini-buses leave from Pazar, the next town, or a visit can be arranged through Trabzon Tourist Office. Çamlıhemsin is a tiny 'alpine' village, 1,219 m up in the mountains; it has four or five basic Swiss-chalet-type guesthouses, and a warm pool in a hut, fed by a thermal spring. People come here from all over Turkey, seeking relief from arthritis, lumbago, rheumatism and goodness knows what else. There are separate bathing sessions for men and women, during which about ten or 15 bodies are crammed into the pool. The warm, mildly sulphurous water is most agreeable.

The drive to Çamlıhemsin follows a raging white river up into the mountains; the road is rough and the trip takes over two hours, but a new road is presently under construction, which promises to ruin what must be one of the most beautiful mountain valleys in the world. The valley is steep, thickly wooded and narrow; here and there ancient pack-horse bridges cross the river, their graceful arches almost a complete circle, creepers hanging from their mossy bricks. Tiny villages and isolated farmsteads perch high on near-vertical cliffs, linked by aerial ropeways and cobbled paths, winding through the woods. Halfway up the road is a village with a primitive suspension bridge and a LOKANTA with a river-balcony, where you can sit and eat fresh rainbow trout. As you climb, the vegetation changes from the tea, figs and hazel of the coast, to beech-forests, rhododendrons, tall firs, bracken and multitudes of wild flowers. Çamlıhemsin itself is the nearest approximation to a mountain-lover's paradise.

The easternmost pass over the mountains starts at HOPA, the last town before the border; it takes you along a high-level route of extraordinary beauty, to ARTVIN. Artvin itself is rather nondescript, but what you come here for is the high mountain plateaux, or *Yayla*. In summer the inhabitants of the villages lower down the mountains move up to the *Yayla* with their cattle, sheep and goats. Many still live in woollen tents, but most have now built *Yayla* villages of brick, stone and wood. Each village has a mosque and perhaps a *Han* or inn, where travellers may stay, eat and drink, in very modest conditions. The main function of the *Han* is as a gathering-place and tea-house for the men of the village; it's the best place to ask directions and information from the locals and to arrange for transport, which in these parts is limited to a space on the back of a lorry.

Up here on the *Yayla*, amongst the meadows and the clouds, are dotted humble little Byzantine and Armenian churches, often in a very good state of preservation. To discover them is an incomparable pleasure, for there will be nobody else around, no tourist facilities, nothing – just the peace and the history and the beauty of the location. It is not within the scope of this book to give directions and routes for these churches, but you can reach the *Yayla* from any one of the points just described: the Zigana Pass, Sumela, Çaykara Pass or Çamlıhemsin; then there's Artvin, and on the road to Erzurum, Yusufeli and Tortum would also be good starting points.

C·H·A·P·T·E·R·10

Practical Information

ELECTRICITY

Standard voltage in Turkey is 220 volts.
Take an adaptor, the sockets may vary
but are generally of the two prong
European type. Supply can be a little
erratic; expect at least one power cut
during your stay.

LAW AND ORDER

There are no police in Turkey, and the
task of enforcing law and order falls to
the *Jandarma* – a division of the army.
These you will see everywhere and they
are generally less formidable than they
look. Certainly they are effective.
Turkey is a very safe country for the
tourist. A combination of the strong
influence of Islam and the military
presence keeps theft and other crimes
at a very low level.

POST OFFICE AND TELEPHONES

You will not fail to notice the bright

yellow and black signs of the Turkish Post Office (PTT). Post boxes are also yellow.There are essentially two different telephone systems. Tokens (*jetons*) which you buy in the PTT are the cheapest, but not the simplest way of making a call. Alternatively, arrange for the connection to be made for you by the PTT staff. This is more expensive, and usually takes a long time, but for international calls, it's usually the better bet. With both systems you need a good deal of patience!

Useful addresses

British Embassy (*Ingiltere Birleşik Kralliğ*)
Şehit Ersan Cad. 46/A
Çankaya
Ankara
Tel: 27 43 10

British Consulate (*Ingiltere Consulate*)
Meşrutiyet Cad. 26
Galatasaray
Istanbul
Tel: 149–8874

American Embassy (*Amerikan Birleşik Devletleri*)
Atatürk Bulvarsı 110
Kavaklıdere
Ankara
Tel: 26 54 70

American Consulate (*Amerikan Consulate*)
Meşrutiyet Cad. 106
Tepebaşi
Beyoğlu
Istanbul
Tel: 145–3220

The addresses given for the following organisations are for head offices only.

Turkish Touring and Automobile Club *(Türkiye Turing ve Otomobil Kurumu)*
Halaskargazi Cad. 364
Şişli
Istanbul
Tel: 52 16 588

Turkish Maritime Lines (*Türkiye Deniscilik Kurumu T.A.O.*)
Rıhtım Cad.
Karaköy
Istanbul
Tel: 44 02 07

Turkish Airlines (*Türk Hava Yolları – THY*)
Abide-i Hürriyet Cad.
Vakif Işhanı, Kat: 2, 154–156
Istanbul

MONEY AND CREDIT CARDS

Coins are rarely used; they're too low in value and anyway, the Turks prefer notes, thick, grubby wads of them. The monetary unit is the Turkish lira (TL).

You can use the most common credit cards in all the major cities and tourist resorts, but don't try to offer your 'flexible friend' to pay for a meal in a country *lokanta*. Travellers' cheques and currency can be changed at any bank (there is no shortage of these in Turkey) and in some of the big hotels.

HEALTH

It is always advisable to take out health insurance when travelling in Turkey. Make sure that it covers Europe and Asia. If you get sick, your hotel will find you a doctor and there's a good chance he'll speak enough English to treat you. *Eczanesi* (Chemists) sell a wide variety of drugs and remedies which you can buy without prescription. Turkish water is all right, but you might as well stick to bottled; it's very cheap anyway. Watch the sun, particularly when tramping round the ruins; sunstroke is unpleasant and can be dangerous – so wear a hat. If anything really serious should occur there are American hospitals in both Istanbul and Ankara, and the general standard of medical treatment for foreigners is good.

FAIRS AND FESTIVALS

Istanbul

End of April to beginning May: Tulip Festival at Emirgan.
Mid-June to mid-July: Istanbul International Arts Festival.

Bursa and Edirne

Early May: Spring Festival, Bursa.
Mid-June: Greased wrestling at Kırkpınar, Edirne.
Mid-July: Bursa International Festival.

Aegean

Early May: International Ephesus Festival, Selçuk.
End of May: Pergamum Festival, Bergama.
Early June: International Mediterranean Festival, Izmir.
Mid-August: Çanakkale Festival of Troy.
End of August: Izmir International Fair.
Early September: Bodrum Festival.
Early September: Çal Wine Festival, Denizli.
Early September: Kuşadasi Festival.

Mediterranean

Mid-May: Silifke Music and Folklore Festival.
End of May: Marmaris Festival.
First week December: St Nicholas Festival, Demre (Antalya).

Inland

Early July: Wrestling, Horse-racing and Javelin-throwing at Konya.
Mid-July: Van Festival of Tourism and Culture.
Mid-September: Cappadocia Wine Festival in Ürgüp and Göreme.
December 14–17:   Mevlana Remembrance Day – the Dervishes whirl at Konya.

MEASUREMENTS

All measurements are given in metric units. For readers more familiar with the imperial system, the accompanying tables are designed to facilitate quick conversion to imperial units. Bold figures in the central columns can be read as either metric or imperial: e.g. 1 kg = 2.20 lb or 1 lb = 0.45 kg.

mm		in	cm		in	m		yds
25.4	1	.039	2.54	1	0.39	0.91	1	1.09
50.8	2	.079	5.08	2	0.79	1.83	2	2.19
76.2	3	.118	7.62	3	1.18	2.74	3	3.28
101.6	4	.157	10.16	4	1.57	3.66	4	4.37
127.0	5	.197	12.70	5	1.97	4.57	5	5.47
152.4	6	.236	15.24	6	2.36	5.49	6	6.56
177.8	7	.276	17.78	7	2.76	6.40	7	7.66
203.2	8	.315	20.32	8	3.15	7.32	8	8.75
228.6	9	.354	22.86	9	3.54	8.23	9	9.84

g		oz		kg		lb		km		miles
28.35	1	.04		0.45	1	2.20		1.61	1	0.62
56.70	2	.07		0.91	2	4.41		3.22	2	1.24
85.05	3	.11		1.36	3	6.61		4.83	3	1.86
113.40	4	.14		1.81	4	8.82		6.44	4	2.48
141.75	5	.18		2.27	5	11.02		8.05	5	3.11
170.10	6	.21		2.72	6	13.23		9.65	6	3.73
198.45	7	.25		3.18	7	15.43		11.26	7	4.35
226.80	8	.28		3.63	8	17.64		12.87	8	4.97
255.15	9	.32		4.08	9	19.84		14.48	9	5.59

ha		acres
0.40	1	2.47
0.81	2	4.94
1.21	3	7.41
1.62	4	9.88
2.02	5	12.36
2.43	6	14.83
2.83	7	17.30
3.24	8	19.77
3.64	9	22.24

Metric to imperial conversion formulae

	multiply by
cm to inches	0.3937
m to feet	3.281
m to yards	1.094
km to miles	0.6214
km^2 to square miles	0.3861
ha to acres	2.471
g to ounces	0.03527
kg to pounds	2.205

BIBLIOGRAPHY

Here are a few books which have contributed a great deal to our enjoyment of Turkey.

One of the most readable and well-informed authors on Turkey is Lord Kinross. We mention three of his books here. *The Ottoman Centuries* (Jonathan Cape, 1977) is a fascinating and comprehensive account of the Ottoman Empire, from Osman's warrior tribe to Atatürk; it's as compulsive and exciting – all 600 pages of it – as a good novel. *Atatürk – Birth of a Nation* (Weidenfeld and Nicolson, 1964) is the best biography of the great man; essential for an understanding of modern Turkey. *Within the Taurus* is a light-hearted account of a journey he made in the 1950s in northern and eastern Turkey.

For an appreciation of the history and the Classical sites of the south and west, you can do no better than George Bean. His three books, *Lycian Turkey* (1978), *Turkey's Southern Shore* (1979) and *Turkey Beyond the Maeander* (1980) are all published by Ernest Benn and are a great help to making sense out of the ruins.

Everyday Life in the Ottoman Empire (Batsford, 1971) by Raphaela Lewis, is a short, well-researched and readable account of what life was like behind the scenes.

Lords of the Golden Horn (Macmillan, 1973) by Noel Barber, concentrates rather more on the sensational aspects of the lives of the sultans, than on their achievements – but it's a good read anyway, and well illustrated.

The Owl's Watchsong (Century, 1986) by J.A. Cuddon. The wanderings and musings of a young man in Istanbul in the 1950s. With wit and elegance he considers a wealth of subjects from 'pole-squatting' and the origins of the eunuch, to storks and the achievements of the Byzantine emperors.

Journey to Kars (Penguin, 1984) by Philip Glazebrook, doesn't tell you much about modern Turkey, but it fills in a lot of interesting and amusing background, and also puts neatly into words everything you've ever thought about travelling but were unable to express.

The Turks (Murray, 1972) by David Hotham. An enthusiastic account of modern Turkey by a perceptive Turcophile.

Blue Guide to Istanbul (Ernest Benn, 1983) by John Freely. John Freely is an authority and an enthusiast on Turkey; this is a very comprehensive guide to Istanbul, written in the form of 20 guided tours in the city and its surroundings.

Türkei 2 (Kohlhammer Reiseführer, 1985) by Vera and Helmut Hell. This is a guide book to the area east of Trabzon. Unfortunately, it is in German, but is full of routes and historical accounts of this fascinating region.

Index

Note: main references are in bold type.

199

INDEX